REGENTS RENAISSANCE DRAMA SERIES

*General Editor:* Cyrus Hoy
*Advisory Editor:* G. E. Bentley

# THE STAPLE OF NEWS

BEN JONSON

# The Staple of News

*Edited by*

DEVRA ROWLAND KIFER

UNIVERSITY OF NEBRASKA PRESS · LINCOLN

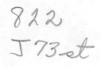

Library of Congress Cataloging in Publication Data
Jonson, Ben, 1573?–1637.
 The staple of news.
 (Regents Renaissance drama series)
 Includes bibliographical references.
 I. Kifer, Devra Rowland, 1927–    ed.
II. Title.
PR2620.A16  1975      822'.3      74–76133
ISBN 0–8032–0295–4

MANUFACTURED IN THE UNITED STATES OF AMERICA

# Regents Renaissance Drama Series

The purpose of the Regents Renaissance Drama Series is to provide soundly edited texts, in modern spelling, of the more significant plays of the Elizabethan, Jacobean, and Caroline theater. Each text in the series is based on a fresh collation of all sixteenth- and seventeenth-century editions. The textual notes, which appear above the line at the bottom of each page, record all substantive departures from the edition used as the copy-text. Variant substantive readings among sixteenth- and seventeenth-century editions are listed there as well. In cases where two or more of the old editions present widely divergent readings, a list of substantive variants in editions through the seventeenth century is given in an appendix. Editions after 1700 are referred to in the textual notes only when an emendation originating in some one of them is received into the text. Variants of accidentals (spelling, punctuation, capitalization) are not recorded in the notes. Contracted forms of characters' names are silently expanded in speech prefixes and stage directions, and, in the case of speech prefixes, are regularized. Additions to the stage directions of the copy-text are enclosed in brackets. Stage directions such as "within" or "aside" are enclosed in parentheses when they occur in the copy-text.

Spelling has been modernized along consciously conservative lines. "Murther" has become "murder," and "burthen," "burden," but within the limits of a modernized text, and with the following exceptions, the linguistic quality of the original has been carefully preserved. The variety of contracted forms (*'em, 'am, 'm, 'um, 'hem*) used in the drama of the period for the pronoun *them* are here regularly given as *'em,* and the alternation between *a'th'* and *o'th'* (for *on* or *of the*) is regularly reproduced as *o'th'*. The copy-text distinction between preterite endings in *-d* and *-ed* is preserved except where the elision of *e* occurs in the penultimate syllable; in such cases, the final syllable is contracted. Thus, where the old editions read "threat'ned," those of the present

v

series read "threaten'd." Where, in the old editions, a contracted preterite in -y'd would yield -i'd in modern spelling (as in "try'd," "cry'd," "deny'd"), the word in here given in its full form (e.g., "tried," "cried," "denied").

Punctuation has been brought into accord with modern practices. The effort here has been to achieve a balance between the generally light pointing of the old editions, and a system of punctuation which, without overloading the text with exclamation marks, semicolons, and dashes, will make the often loosely flowing verse (and prose) of the original syntactically intelligible to the modern reader. Dashes are regularly used only to indicate interrupted speeches, or shifts of address within a single speech.

Explanatory notes, chiefly concerned with glossing obsolete words and phrases, are printed below the textual notes at the bottom of each page. References to stage directions in the notes follow the admirable system of the Revels editions, whereby stage directions are keyed, decimally, to the line of the text before or after which they occur. Thus, a note on 0.2 has reference to the second line of the stage direction at the beginning of the scene in question. A note on 115.1 has reference to the first line of the stage direction following line 115 of the text of the relevant scene.

CYRUS HOY

University of Rochester

# Contents

# List of Abbreviations

conj.  conjecture

Cunningham *The Works of Ben Jonson.* Ed. William Gifford, with notes by Francis Cunningham. 9 vols. London, 1875.

de Winter *The Staple of News.* Ed. de Winter. Yale Studies in English, vol. 28. New York, 1905.

F *The Workes of Benjamin Jonson: The Second Volume.* London, 1640.

F3 *The Works of Ben Jonson.* London, 1692.

Frank Joseph Frank. *The Beginnings of the English Newspaper, 1620–1660.* Cambridge, Mass., 1961.

Gifford *The Works of Ben Jonson.* Ed. William Gifford. 9 vols. London, 1816.

H.S. *Ben Jonson.* Ed. C. H. Herford, Percy and Evelyn Simpson. 11 vols. Oxford, 1925–52.

Knights L. C. Knights. *Drama and Society in the Age of Jonson.* London, 1937.

Linthicum M. Channing Linthicum. *Costume in the Drama of Shakespeare and His Contemporaries.* Oxford, 1936.

Markham Gervase Markham. *Country Contentments, or the English Huswife.* London, 1623.

Nares Robert Nares. *A Glossary.* Ed. J. O. Halliwell and Thomas Wright. London, 1882.

OED *Oxford English Dictionary*

Partridge A. C. Partridge. *The Accidence of Ben Jonson's Plays, Masques, and Entertainments.* Cambridge, 1953.

Pliny Pliny. *Natural History.* Vol. 3. Trans. H. Rackham. Loeb Classical Library. Cambridge, Mass., and London, 1956.

ix

Ray · · · · · John Ray. *A Collection of English Proverbs.* Cambridge, 1678.

S.D. · · · · stage direction

S.P. · · · · speech prefix

Stow · · · · John Stow. *A Survey of London,* 1598, 1603. 2 vols. Ed. C. L. Kingsford. Oxford, 1908.

Sugden · · · Edward H. Sugden. *A Topographical Dictionary of the Works of Shakespeare and His Fellow Dramatists.* Manchester, 1925.

Tilley · · · · Morris Palmer Tilley. *A Dictionary of the Proverbs in England in the Sixteenth and Seventeenth Centuries.* Ann Arbor, 1950.

Whalley · · · *The Workes of Ben Jonson.* Ed. Peter Whalley. 7 vols. London, 1756.

1716 · · · · *The Workes of Ben Jonson.* 6 vols. London, 1716.

# Introduction

## THE PLAY

"And I have hope to erect a Staple for news ere long," says the Factor in Jonson's masque *News from the New World Discovered in the Moon*, "whither all shall be brought and thence again vented under the name of Staple news." Six years later, in 1626, that Staple was erected, stocked with news, gullers, and gulls, and brought forth upon the stage by the King's Men.

Satires of the burgeoning newsmongering industry were common in the seventeenth century in dramatic and nondramatic literature.[1] Nowhere, however, is there the full-blown satire that Jonson incorporated in *The Staple of News*.

For Jonson the notion of the News Office afforded some of the same opportunities for comical satire as another social institution, *Bartholomew Fair*. Like the Fair, the News Office is depicted as a place where the gullible are fleeced and the thirst for novelty and hunger for money are satisfied; in addition, a good time can be had by an audience that feels morally superior to the gullers and intellectually superior to the gulled.

From *News from the New World*, Jonson took not only the notion of a monopolistic news service that purveys nonsensical news but also much of the dialogue between Pennyboy Junior and the officers of the Staple in Act I. The news, however, is new. Much had happened in the world since 1620, and Jonson's news bristles with topical allusions.

---

1. The best-known examples are in Fletcher's *The Fair Maid of the Inn*, Shirley's *The Schoole of Complement*, Lupton's *London and the Countrey Carbonadoed*, and Brathwaite's *Whimsies*. Modern scholarship indicates that most early criticism was unjustified, that the news was as accurate as it could be under the circumstances. Jonson's portrayal of the News Office staff as confidence men rather than as newsmen is amusing but, we are told, wholly inaccurate. See, for example, Joseph Frank, *The Beginnings of the English Newspaper, 1620–1660* (Cambridge, Mass., 1961), pp. 12–13.

The Staple is not only a specific satire on newsmongering and a general satire on gulls and gullibility, it is also a depiction and criticism of contemporary economic practices. The Staple is set up as a monopoly,

> Where all the news of all sorts shall be brought,
> And there be examin'd, and then register'd,
> And so be issu'd under the seal of the Office,
> As Staple News, no other news be current.
>
> (I.ii.33–36)

The governor of the Staple has "projected" it (I.ii.42). News is the staple or "commodity" (I.ii.51) which arrives "three bale together" (I.v.143). In *News from the New World,* news was free to all who had ears; in the Staple Office it is available only in exchange for pennies and pounds.

The language of monopolies and projects was all too familiar to Londoners, who had been angered by King James's revival of the Elizabethan practice of granting monopolies indiscriminately. In 1626, "the City was just recovering from the worst depression in living memory."[2] Jonson's audience could call to mind such recent economic fiascoes as Alderman Cockayne's cloth-finishing scheme, a project that was expected to add £300,000 a year to the country's income but instead, they believed, contributed importantly to the ensuing depression.[3]

So much for the institution of the Staple, but what of the commodity itself, the news? The first that we hear of news in the play is Mistress Tattle's warning to the Prologue: "Look your news be new and fresh, Master Prologue, and untainted. I shall find them else, if they be stale or fly-blown, quickly" (Induction, ll. 24–26). As the play proceeds, she carries out this threat. After the great Staple scene of Act III with its outpouring of news gathered from the four corners of the earth, she complains: "I have had better news from the bake-house by ten

---

2. Menna Prestwich, *Cranfield: Politics and Profits under the Early Stuarts* (Oxford, 1966), p. 165.

3. L. C. Knights, *Drama & Society in the Age of Jonson* (London, 1937), p. 211.

thousand parts, in a morning, or the conduits in Westminster"
(Intermean III.19–21). She much prefers the gossip of West-
minster, "true or no," to the commodity of the Office (Intermean
III.37).

The news itself, as Jonson was later to observe, is not "any
reasonable man's" (To the Readers, l. 8): Galileo has invented
a burning glass that may be ignited by moonshine in order to
destroy any fleet at sea; the King of Spain was made Pope and
Holy Emperor on the thirtieth of February: "a colony of cooks"
is off to America to convert the cannibals and make them "good,
eating Christians" (III.ii.155–58). There is news of Pennyboy
Junior, the Golden Heir, news of the theater, news that the
Catholic League is winning in the Thirty Years War or, if the
buyer prefers, news that the Protestant Union is winning. There
is news, and news, and more news, and the claims for their
authenticity are equivocal. Fitton, whose very name means lie,
says of the news being vented, "All are alike true and certain"
(III.ii.27). When even the credulous Pennyboy Junior begins
to doubt and asks, "Is't true?" Fitton's reply is, "As true as the
rest" (III.ii.93).

The satiric nature of the Staple of News is clear: In The
Prologue for the Court, Jonson says unequivocally, "Although
our title, sir, be *News,/* We yet adventure here to tell you none."
Instead, he says, the audience will see "common follies" as close
to truth "as fant'sy could them state/ Or poetry, without scandal,
imitate." But the role of the Staple in the play as a whole is
very difficult to assess. Jonson has written uproariously funny
dialogue in the great Staple scene, which he placed at the physical
center of the play. Much of the dialogue and action of Acts I
and II is pointed toward this scene, in which Pecunia is finally
lured to the Office. Yet when Act III is over, we see no more of
the Staple. Perhaps the joke had been exploited to the full.
Perhaps the potential humor in an imaginary news office, unlike
that of an actual fair, could not sustain an entire play. It is
impossible to reconstruct Jonson's reasons for, in Gossip Expectation's words, letting the Staple "fall most abruptly" (Intermean
IV.74), but the result of his decision is to disappoint the expecta-
tions of the reader and to assign to the Office a secondary place
in the play.

Despite the promise of the title of the play, its plot is far more concerned with the adventures of Pennyboy Junior than with the rise and fall of the Staple; the play begins and ends with him. In the Persons of the Play, Jonson describes Young Pennyboy as "the son, the heir and suitor"; neither here nor elsewhere do we learn his given name. His candid and outspoken father, who is named Francis, is appropriately known as Frank. His avaricious, usurious uncle, called Richer, is "not Richard, but old Harry Pennyboy" (II.iv.201). Again the name is appropriate, for Old Harry is a familiar name for the Devil.

The story of Pennyboy Junior is in part a morality play. It is a story of Every-Heir as he at first yields to the false temptations of the world and finally recognizes them for what they are and eschews them. Like *Everyman,* the play is limited to a single day in the hero's life. Unlike Everyman, but like later, secular morality heroes, Pennyboy Junior needs to learn how to live well rather than how to die well.

When first we see Pennyboy Junior, he has just come into his inheritance. He is heir to £60,000, an income of £2,000 a year. Much of the opening scenes is taken up with his trying on his expensive, ultramodish new clothes and admiring his appearance. There is a clear conspiracy among the tradesmen to fleece him; his pockets alone cost £12. During the first four acts, he squanders hundreds of pounds, and as the fifth act opens, he is back in his lodgings, again looking in his mirror, but this time wearing a beggar's tattered cloak. By an "act of piety and good affection" (V.iii.23), he finally redeems himself and is then allowed to put off his rags and be himself again with the implicit understanding that there will be no more twelve-pound pockets.

Jonson deliberately uses many morality-play devices. The character of Pecunia, for example, and her entourage of Wax, Band (Bond), Mortgage, Statute, and Broker are clearly abstractions appropriate to a morality play. In the Intermean that follows Act II the gossips speak of the play as a morality: Mistress Mirth asks how the ladies like "the Vice i'the play," whom she identifies as "old Covetousness, the sordid Pennyboy" (Intermean II.6–8). Tattle does not agree with Mirth's characterization of Pennyboy Senior; there's no devil in the play to carry him off to hell, she argues, and he has no wooden dagger: "I'd not give a rush for a Vice that has not a wooden dagger to snap at everybody he meets" (ll. 11–13). Mirth, the most sophisticated playgoer of the group, tells her that her standards are somewhat old-fashioned: "That was the old way, gossip, when Iniquity came in like Hokos Pokos in a juggler's jerkin, with false skirts, like the knave of clubs! But now they are attir'd like men and women o'the time, the Vices, male and female!" Here are "Prodigality, like a young heir, and his mistress Money (whose favors he scatters like counters), prank'd up like a prime lady . . ." (ll. 14–20).

Pennyboy Senior is not the kind of Vice that Tattle speaks of. He is not the amusing, sprightly intriguer of the late moralities. The Vice character had taken a turn for the worse in more recent drama. The character had developed into the very articulate, conscienceless, self-proclaimed villainous manipulator exemplified brilliantly by Shakespeare's Iago and Edmund. It is this kind of "Vice" character that Jonson does use in the play, the scheming lawyer Picklock. Having plotted first with Pennyboy Canter to draw up and execute his will although he was not dead, then plotting with Pennyboy Junior to obtain Pecunia for him and with Cymbal to obtain Pecunia for him, Picklock finally plots to cheat them all. In the moment he is alone on stage, he announces and relishes his villainous intentions:

> If I can now commit father and son
> And make my profits out of both, commence
> A suit with the old man for his whole state
> And go to law with the son's credit, undo
> Both, both with their own money, it were a piece
> Worthy my nightcap and the gown I wear.
>
> (V.i.99–104)

Since the *Staple* is comedy not tragedy, Picklock's crimes are not so great as those of Iago and Edmund, yet the resemblance is unmistakable.

In the earliest moralities, before the development of the Vice with his dagger of lath, all seven Vices or Sins were often among the characters. A number of these vices figure importantly here. Pennyboy Junior is puffed up with Pride as he looks at himself in his new clothes and wishes that time would stand still. As Mirth observes, Pennyboy Senior is indeed Covetousness, as it takes the form of Avarice. The jeerers epitomize Covetousness in the form of Envy. Gluttony and Lust, "the fury of men's gullets and their groins" (III.iv.46) in Pennyboy Senior's phrase, also figure in the play..

The peculiarly Jonsonian use of morality play devices may best be seen in Act IV, which takes place at St. Dunstan's Tavern in the room called Apollo. It is usual in morality plays to lay the great temptation scene in a tavern, a microcosm of the World and the temptations of the Flesh. Jonson uses a very special tavern here: Apollo is the meeting place of Jonson and those who sealed themselves of the Tribe of Ben. Here Pennyboy Junior is not tempted to ordinary debauchery; he is tempted to a Jonsonian cardinal sin, the abuse of language. And for a moment he yields.

Before the scenes in the tavern, Pennyboy Junior had already demonstrated the ease with which he could be led into abusing the language or accepting its abuse by others. His first speeches are a pastiche of commonplaces. Like the other gulls, he willingly swallows the baits that are laid in the Staple Office, accepting patent falsehoods as though they were truths. In the tavern, he joins the jeerers in their gratuitous insult matches. One by one, Pennyboy Canter demonstrates that the jeerers are canters. When Piedmantle finishes reading Pecunia's blazon, Pennyboy Canter turns to his son and asks, "Is not this canting? Do you understand him?" Pennyboy Junior's reply is "Not I. But it sounds well . . ." (IV.iv.27–28). In the manner of W. S. Gilbert's patter songs, Pennyboy Canter then goes on to recite catalogues of terms and phrases used by Almanac, Shunfield, and Madrigal in order to demonstrate that they too are canters. He concludes his most brilliant exposé, his recital of the mint-phrases of the courtier, by observing that " 'tis the worst of canting/ By how much it affects the sense it has not" (IV.iv.74–75). Despite Pennyboy Canter's ruthless exposure of the pretensions of the jeerers, Pennyboy Junior decides not to turn away from his evil companions but instead to use his inheritance to perpetuate and propagate their skills by setting up and endowing a college for canters.[4]

Unlike the Good Angel or the Virtues of a morality play, Pennyboy Canter, having revealed his true identity, gives the assemblage a terrible tongue-lashing, takes Pecunia from Pennyboy Junior, and bids his son farewell:

> Farewell, my beggar in velvet, for today.
>
> *He points him to his patch'd cloak thrown off.*
>
> Tomorrow you may put on that grave robe
> And enter your great work of Canters' College,
> Your work and worthy of a chronicle.
>
> (IV.iv.176–79)

As Jonson creates his own eighth cardinal sin, he also leaves his peculiar impress on the biblical story of the Prodigal Son, a common motif in Tudor drama.[5] Since Jonson is concerned in part with a scrupulous adherence to the unity of time and action, he reduces to a single day the vague but lengthy period in which the biblical Prodigal Son "wasted his substance with riotous living" (Luke 15:13). The message of Christian love and rejoicing at the sinner returned is completely absent from Jonson's version. Pennyboy Junior's repentance is only part of the price he must pay to be reinstated in *his* father's good graces. He must also outwit Picklock and demonstrate his worth and loyalty to his father in practical ways before a reconciliation is possible.

---

4. Richard Levin analyzes the abuse of language common to the News Office, the jeerers, and the projected college in "*The Staple of News,* The Society of Jeerers, and Canters' College," *Philological Quarterly* 44 (1965):445–53.

5. As late as 1605, an anonymous comedy called *The London Prodigal* was published. In his edition of *The Staple of News* (New York, 1905), de Winter argued for that play as a source. There is only one demonstrable similarity between the plays, and that is the father who announces his own death and then acts as his son's follower. *The London Prodigal* covers a long period of time in which young Flowerdale is guilty of viciously evil behavior before he repents and is forgiven.

In considering the play as partly satire and partly morality, no accounting has been made of the very large role played by Pennyboy Senior. If he were only one of many vices to be anatomized, a disproportionate amount of the play is devoted to him. Nor is his role adequately explained by asserting that his abuse of money, because it is antithetical to Pennyboy Junior's, allows Pecunia and Jonson to preach the virtues of "the golden mean" (V.vi.64).[6] It is only when we consider the play as a festive celebration, a holiday play, that his role becomes clear.[7]

It is Mistress Mirth who sets the tone of the entertainment, and Pennyboy Senior is her antithesis. As Pennyboy Canter points out to his son, if the uncle were to accompany the others to the tavern, he would "spoil all your mirth" (II.v.125).

Clearly Jonson has invited playgoers to the theater not only for the didactic purpose he announces in The Prologue for the Stage but also that they may be mirthful and take a holiday from the workaday world. A number of specific references in the play indicate that it is written in celebration of Shrovetide, the last days of indulgence before the abstinence of the Lenten season. Mirth is, she says, "the daughter of Christmas and spirit of Shrovetide" (Induction, ll. 11–12). In keeping with the season, she tells us that when she saw the poet-playwright back-

6. The use of a clearly schematized antithesis of the two extreme abuses of money may be found in the late morality play *The Contention between Liberality and Prodigality*, 1602. Despite its title, the play actually opposes Tenacity and Prodigality. A. B. Stonex, in "The Sources of Jonson's *The Staple of News*," *PMLA* 30 (1915):821–30, argues that *The Contention* is a source of the allegory, main situation, and moral in *The Staple of News*. Although there are some similarities, the relation cannot be demonstrated. The two lines that Herford and Simpson, in their edition of Jonson's works (*Ben Jonson* [Oxford, 1925–52], 10:259), quote as identical in both plays are in fact to be found only in Jonson.

7. Much of the following discussion is indebted to Chapters 4, 7, and 8 of C. L. Barber's *Shakespeare's Festive Comedy* (Princeton, 1959). One resemblance between *The Staple of News* and Nashe's pageant *Summer's Last Will and Testament*, which Barber considers a prototype of festive comedy, is pointed out by C. R. Baskervill: "The gossips of *The Staple of News* . . . are to my mind distinctly modeled on Nashe's device of Will Summer" (*English Elements in Jonson's Early Comedy* [Austin, Texas, 1911], p. 148).

stage, "rolling himself up and down like a tun," she was put "in mind of a good Shroving-dish" (Induction, ll. 59–63). The eel boats have come from Holland to supply food for Lent (III.ii.84–85). Mirth hopes that the butter will be appropriate "to the time of year, in Lent, delicate almond butter" (Intermean II.63). The jeerers threaten Pennyboy Senior with the possibility of his turning into a Jack-a-Lent (V.v.35), the puppet figure that was set up to be pelted from Ash Wednesday to Good Friday and then burned.

More interesting than these specific references is the treatment of festive ritual in the play.[8] Shrove Tuesday was carnival time, a time for revelry to indicate that there would soon be a "putting away of flesh (as food)."[9] There is much talk of good eating in the play. Lickfinger the cook enjoys a universally fine reputation. He can turn funeral stew meats into so great a delight that the guests rejoice as though "the funeral feast/ Had been a wedding dinner" (III.iii.33–34). The procession of food is almost endless: an olla podrida, game, fish, poultry, custards, pies, relishes, sauces, almond paste.

In the midst of such gastronomic delights, Pennyboy Senior is set as an abstemious kill-joy. He has no use for food except as he may sell whatever gifts of food he receives. He rails against gluttony, not in fact because it is sinful but because of the money that it wastes.

Who can endure to see
The fury of men's gullets . . .
What fires, what cooks, what kitchens might be spar'd?
What stews, ponds, parks, coops, garners, magazines . . . .
(III.iv.45–48)

He begrudges himself so much that he does not even allow himself to dream of a good meal. He preserves himself, as he boasts, "Like an old hoary rat, with moldy piecrust" (II.i.18).

8. I have presented a detailed analysis of *The Staple* as festive comedy in "*The Staple of News:* Jonson's Festive Comedy," *SEL* 12 (1972):329-344.

9. *OED,* from the medieval Latin *carnem levare.*

Even when his nephew invites him to dine as his guest, he refuses.

Good drink too is part of the festivities of Shrovetide; Bacchus was a traditional subject for verses assigned to Eton boys on Shrove Monday. Good drink is also part of the festivity of the play, and again Pennyboy Senior is opposed to such festive celebration. In sending Broker to keep watch over Pecunia as she dines in Apollo with Pennyboy Junior, he orders him to "serve in Apollo but take heed of Bacchus" (III.iv.17). Broker does not heed this injunction, and when Pennyboy Senior comes to Apollo to seek him, Broker is dead drunk. Lickfinger offers Pennyboy Senior some sack, but he strikes the cup from the cook's hand and the wine is spilled on the floor.

Pennyboy Senior's opposition is not limited to the festival spirit of the play. He is opposed to all things that give life to the community and the community is agreed—even the boys, who break his windows—in opposing him. He is the only character in the play who is universally despised, by the characters in the play proper and by the gossips. He does not know how to use life or money. For the sympathetic characters of the play, "use" means "enjoy." For Pennyboy Senior it means "to take interest" or "practice usury." By the end of the play, he has suffered madness and reformed. He declares a new holiday and gives his servants "their year and day of jubilee" (V.vi.53). His last speech announces his complete reformation and a new festivity. He will go to cleanse his vices, Pennyboy Junior will inherit all his goods, and Pecunia will be given in marriage to Pennyboy Junior.[10]

Of the characters in the play proper, it is Pennyboy Junior who best exemplifies the spirit of holiday. His life for the first four acts is a universal wish-fulfillment. He has a great deal of

10. Since completing the preparation of this edition, I have reached the conclusion that Pennyboy Senior was initially intended as a full-length caricature of the eminent jurist Sir Edward Coke and that the passage in the last scene in which Pennyboy Senior punningly identifies Lickfinger with Coke was added before the play was printed in order to protect Jonson against a charge of libel. The argument is set forth in detail in an article entitled "Too Many Cookes: An Addition to the Printed Version of Jonson's *Staple of Newes*," *English Language Notes* 11 (1974):264–71.

money which he has in no way earned. There is no one to say him nay at any turn. His is a world of good food and drink, expensive clothes, fabulously wealthy and willing princesses, and no responsibilities. Now that he is twenty-one, he wants time to stop so that this holidaying can go on forever. He wants, in the words of another reformed prodigal, "all the year" to be "playing holidays," and Jonson in the person of Pennyboy Canter knows that the year is made up primarily of everydays. Pennyboy Junior has his holiday, short-lived but intense, and then the world, in the person of his father, must make him fit to live in the everyday world. Like that other prodigal, Shakespeare's Prince Hal, he must learn to seek out "good and virtuous persons" (IV.iv.135), to live with "sound mind" (V.vi. 66), and to pursue a moderate, workable, everyday course.

The holidaying playgoers, Mistresses Mirth, Tattle, Expectation, and Censure, have acted as a Chorus for the first four acts. They have enjoyed holiday license in being allowed to mock the poet and his play. In the final resolution of the action, however, there is no place for them. Their world is a topsy-turvy one. Except for their intense dislike of Pennyboy Senior, all their responses are inappropriate to what Jonson considers the real world. They cannot abide the virtuous, articulate, moral Canter and demand an apology from him and from the poet for putting an end to Pennyboy Junior's riotous living. They are delighted by Pennyboy Junior's rash spending and his plans for founding Canters' College. Despite Pennyboy Canter's demonstration of the immorality and hollowness of the jeerers, Censure has fallen in love with Fitton, Expectation is enamored of Almanac, and Tattle admires Picklock's great learning. All the gossips want the Canter to be punished while all the vicious and immoral characters thrive. As the play ends, there is no place for the inverted values of the gossips. The jeerers have been routed, Pennyboy Junior and Pennyboy Senior have reformed, the News Office has vanished, and the rational, everyday world is again in control.[11]

11. Lengthy discussions of the play may be found in two recent general studies of Jonson: Calvin G. Thayer, *Ben Jonson: Studies in the Plays* (Norman, Okla., 1963) and Robert Knoll, *Ben Jonson's Plays: An Introduction* (Lincoln, Nebr., 1964). *The Staple of News* is dis-

## DATE AND TEXT

The only authoritative text for *The Staple of News* is the folio printed in 1631 by John Beale for Robert Allot. The play was entered on the Stationers' Register to John Waterson on April 14, 1626, shortly after its performance by the King's Men. Despite Jonson's apparent decision to publish it, nothing more is heard of the play until September 7, 1631, when Waterson's rights were transferred to Robert Allot. In 1631, a slim folio volume containing *Bartholomew Fair, The Devil is an Ass,* and *The Staple of News* was distributed to a few of Jonson's patrons and friends.

In 1640, Richard Meighen issued what the title page describes as "The Second Volume of Jonson's Works," in which the three plays were included. Meighen apparently used sheets he had purchased from John Legatt and Andrew Crooke, who had in turn purchased them from Allot's widow. The title page of *The Staple* carries a publication date of 1631.

The play, like John Beale's other work, is carelessly printed. There are obvious errors of omitted letters and words, misspellings, incorrect attributions of speeches, and misnumbered scenes. There is no doubt that the sheets were not proofread by Jonson; there is some doubt that they were proofread by anyone. There are almost no variants in the extant copies, but as Herford and Simpson point out,[12] there are a few minor but inexplicable corrections: F4 recto—"moyetie" is italicized, and a comma is inserted after "paths"; F4 verso—"tyssues" is corrected to "tissues."

The most striking peculiarity of the text is the great number of marginal notes. Jonson's usual practice was to place a few explanatory notes and stage directions in the margins of his

cussed also in Edward B. Partridge, "The Symbolism of Clothes in Jonson's Last Plays," *JEGP* 56 (1957):396–409. For discussions that make avarice and money the focus of the play see Helena Watts Baum, *The Satiric & the Didactic in Ben Jonson's Comedy* (Chapel Hill, N.C., 1947), Freda L. Townsend, *Apologie for Bartholmew Fayre* (New York, 1947), John J. Enck, *Jonson and the Comic Truth* (Madison, Wisc., 1957), and Edward B. Partridge, *The Broken Compass: A Study of the Major Comedies of Ben Jonson* (New York, 1958).

12. *Ben Jonson,* 6:276.

plays, but *The Devil is an Ass* and *The Staple of News* have a great number of side notes that simply restate the action or the dialogue. In some passages there are so many notes that they comprise a summary or scenario of that part of the play. Gifford felt that these notes were not Jonson's and simply deleted them; no other editor has doubted their authenticity. In any event it is at least as difficult to explain why the printer would have added them as it is to explain why Jonson himself wrote them.

Jonson added a note "To The Readers" to the printed version, and there is good reason to believe that at least one other passage (V.vi.42–48) was added or changed after the play was acted. The lines in which the reformed Pennyboy Senior uses a good deal of legal terminology and identifies Lickfinger punningly with Sir Edward Coke are meaningful only after the beginning of the 1628 session of Parliament, when Coke took a stand against committing prisoners without bail as being against the liberty of the subject.[13]

The collation is Aa recto, title page; Aa verso, the Persons of the Play; Aa2 recto and verso, the Induction; Aa3 recto, the Prologue for the Stage; Aa3 verso, the Prologue for the Court; Aa4, BbC4 (signature letters shift from double to single at C3), D–H4, I–I6, the text of the play, I6 verso, Epilogue. The play is paged continuously from pages [1], 2–75, [76] with pages 19, 22, and 63 misnumbered 9, 16, 36, respectively).

Three copies of the play in the Harvard University Library (two of the 1640 edition, F, and one of the 1692 edition, F3) and two copies in the British Museum (one F and one F3) have been collated for this edition. The annotations of the Herford and Simpson edition have of course proved of great value.

A Skidmore College research grant was very helpful in the preparation of this edition. I am deeply grateful to my poet friend Laurence Josephs for many hours of valuable conversation about the play and to Patricia-Ann Lee for her help with the explanatory notes on Stuart history.

Devra Rowland Kifer

Saratoga Springs, N.Y.

13. See footnote 10 above.

# THE STAPLE OF NEWS

# THE PERSONS OF THE PLAY

PENNYBOY [JUNIOR], *the son, the heir and suitor*
PENNYBOY [CANTER], *the father, the canter*
PENNYBOY [SENIOR], *the uncle, the usurer*
CYMBAL, *Master of the Staple and prime jeerer*
FITTON, *emissary [to] Court and jeerer*                     5
ALMANAC, *doctor in physic and jeerer*
SHUNFIELD, *sea captain and jeerer*
MADRIGAL, *poetaster and jeerer*
PICKLOCK, *man o'law and emissary [to] Westminster*
PIEDMANTLE, *pursuivant at arms and heraldet*               10
REGISTER, *of the Staple or Office*
NATHANIEL, *first clerk of the Office*
THOMAS BARBER, *second clerk of the Office*
PECUNIA, *Infanta of the Mines*
MORTGAGE, *her nurse*                                        15
STATUTE, *[her] first woman*
BAND, *[her] second woman*
[ROSE] WAX, *[her] chambermaid*
BROKER, *secretary and gentleman-usher to her Grace*
LICKFINGER, *a master-cook and parcel-poet*                 20

7. and jeerer] *F; a* Jerrer *F3*.

---

2. *Canter*] beggar or vagabond, one who uses the cant of thieves or beggars.
   4. *Cymbal*] whose lack of charity accounts for his name (1 Corinthians 13:1); he is called "tinkling" captain in V.vi.8.
   5. *Fitton*] fitten, lie, *v.* or *sb.*
   5. *emissary*] See I.ii.47, note.
   7. *Shunfield*] *field* meaning both battle and land.
   8. *Madrigal*] Jonson mocks this popular form in *Epicoene*, II.iii.24–40. All Jonson citations are from the Herford and Simpson edition.
   10. *Pursuivant . . . heraldet*] junior heraldic officer and petty herald; the pursuivants, the third and lowest level of heralds of the College of Arms, are Rouge Dragon, Blue Mantle, Portcullis, and Rouge Croix.
   12. *Nathaniel*] the stationer (publishing bookseller) Nathaniel Butter.
   17. *Band*] bond, security given.
   19. *secretary*] one entrusted with the secrets of another.
   20. *Lickfinger*] from the proverb: "He is an ill cook that cannot lick his own fingers" (Tilley, C 636).
   20. *parcel-poet*] partly poet.

## THE PERSONS OF THE PLAY

FASHIONER, *the tailor of the times*
LINENER
HABERDASHER
[LEATHERLEG, *a*] *shoemaker*
SPURRIER                                                    25
CUSTOMERS, *male and female*
PORTER, TWO DOGS[, FIDDLERS, NICHOLAS, *the boy*
PROLOGUE
GOSSIP MIRTH
GOSSIP TATTLE                                               30
GOSSIP EXPECTATION
GOSSIP CENSURE]

The Scene, *London*

---

21. *Fashioner*] tailor.
22. *Linener*] shirt-maker.
23. *Haberdasher*] hatter.

# THE INDUCTION

*The* Prologue *enters. After him,* Gossip Mirth, Gossip Tattle, Gossip Expectation, *and* Gossip Censure, *four gentlewomen lady-like attired.*

PROLOGUE.

For your own sake, not ours—

MIRTH.

Come, gossip, be not asham'd. The play is *The Staple of News,* and you are the mistress and lady of Tattle, let's ha' your opinion of it. Do you hear, gentleman? What are you, gentleman-usher to the play? Pray you help us      5
to some stools here.

PROLOGUE.

Where? O'the stage, ladies?

MIRTH.

Yes, o'the stage. We are persons of quality, I assure you, and women of fashion, and come to see and to be seen. My gossip Tattle here, and gossip Expectation, and my      10
gossip Censure, and I am Mirth, the daughter of Christmas and spirit of Shrovetide. They say, "It's merry when gossips meet." I hope your play will be a merry one.

---

2–3. *The Staple of News*] Jonson had apparently conceived this notion much earlier; in *News from the New World Discovered in the Moon,* 1620, the Factor hoped "to erect a Staple of newes ere long" (ll. 45–46).

7. *O'the stage*] Among the many criticisms of playgoers, usually men, sitting on the stage are the Induction of *Cynthia's Revels* and Chap. 6, "How a Gallant should behave himself in a Play-house," in Dekker's *The Guls Horne-booke.*

12. *Shrovetide*] the three days immediately preceding Ash Wednesday.

12–13. *"It's merry . . . meet."*] proverbial (Tilley, G 382); *'Tis Merry When Gossips Meet,* 1602, is a satiric poem by Samuel Rowlands.

PROLOGUE.

Or you will make it such, ladies. Bring a form here.

*[A bench is brought in.]*

But what will the noblemen think, or the grave wits    15
here, to see you seated on the bench thus?

MIRTH.

Why, what should they think, but that they had mothers,
as we had, and those mothers had gossips (if their children were christen'd) as we are, and such as had a longing
to see plays and sit upon them, as we do, and arraign    20
both them and their poets?

PROLOGUE.

Oh, is that your purpose? Why, Mistress Mirth and
Madame Tattle, enjoy your delights freely.

TATTLE.

Look your news be new and fresh, Master Prologue, and
untainted. I shall find them else, if they be stale or    25
fly-blown, quickly.

PROLOGUE.

We ask no favor from you. Only we would entreat of
Madam Expectation—

EXPECTATION.

What, Master Prologue?

PROLOGUE.

That your ladyship would expect no more than you    30
understand.

EXPECTATION.

Sir, I can expect enough.

PROLOGUE.

I fear, too much lady, and teach others to do the like.

EXPECTATION.

I can do that too if I have cause.

14.1] *Gifford.*

---

18. *gossips*] godmothers; elsewhere the word has its modern, general
meaning.

20. *arraign*] judge, try.

30–31. *expect . . . understand*] a recurrent criticism Jonson makes
of his audience; see III.ii 301–302, and *Neptune's Triumph*, l. 61.

PROLOGUE.

    Cry you mercy, you never did wrong but with just cause.   35
What's this lady?

MIRTH.

    Curiosity, my lady Censure.

PROLOGUE.

    Oh, Curiosity! You come to see who wears the new suit
today, whose clothes are best penn'd whatever the part
be, which actor has the best leg and foot, what king   40
plays without cuffs and his queen without gloves, who
rides post in stockings and dances in boots?

CENSURE.

    Yes, and which amorous prince makes love in drink or
does overact prodigiously in beaten satin and, having
got the trick on't, will be monstrous still, in despite   45
of counsel.

BOOKHOLDER [*within*].

    Mend your lights, gentlemen. Master Prologue, begin.

       *The Tiremen enter to mend the lights.*

TATTLE.

    Ay me!

EXPECTATION.

    Who's that?

47.1] *Gifford.*

---

    35. *Cry . . . cause*] Caesar's reply to Metellus Cimber, *Julius Caesar*,
III.i.47–48, "Know, Caesar doth not wrong nor without cause/ Will
he be satisfied" is quoted in *Timber*, l. 664, as "Caesar did never
wrong, but with just cause." In this famous criticism of Shakespeare,
Jonson instances this line as one which "could not escape laughter."
(The discrepancy between these readings is discussed by J. Dover
Wilson in "Ben Jonson and *Julius Caesar*," *Shakespeare Survey* 2
[1949]: 38–42.)
    39. *penn'd*] feathered.
    44. *beaten*] embroidered.
    47. S. P. *Bookholder*] prompter.
    47. *lights*] Although the private theaters (in this instance Black-
friars), unlike the public playhouses, used artificial illumination,
lights were used here to indicate that the scene takes place in the
early morning.
    47.1. *Tiremen*] dressers, property men.

PROLOGUE.

Nay, start not, ladies. These carry no fireworks to fright 50
you, but a torch i'their hands to give light to the
business. The truth is, there are a set of gamesters
within in travail of a thing call'd a play and would fain
be deliver'd of it, and they have entreated me to be
their man-midwife, the Prologue, for they are like to 55
have a hard labor on't.

TATTLE.

Then the poet has abus'd himself, like an ass, as he is.

MIRTH.

No, his actors will abuse him enough, or I am deceiv'd.
Yonder he is within (I was i'the tiring-house awhile to
see the actors dress'd) rolling himself up and down like 60
a tun i'the midst of 'em, and spurges. Never did vessel
of wort or wine work so! His sweating put me in mind
of a good Shroving-dish (and I believe would be taken
up for a service of state somewhere, an't were known),
a stew'd poet! He doth sit like an unbrac'd drum with 65
one of his heads beaten out. For that you must note, a
poet hath two heads as a drum has (one for making,
the other repeating), and his repeating head is all to
pieces. They may gather it up i'the tiring-house, for
he hath torn the book in a poetical fury and put himself 70
to silence in dead sack, which, were there no other
vexation, were sufficient to make him the most miserable
emblem of patience.

CENSURE.

The Prologue, peace.

---

53. *fain*] gladly.
57. *abus'd . . . ass*] sexual innuendo imposed on the proverb: "He
is an ass that hurts himself" (Tilley, A 377).
59. *tiring-house*] dressing room.
61. *spurges*] froths or foams.
62. *wort*] unfermented beer.
63–64. *taken up*] borrowed.
65. *unbrac'd drum*] drum with the tension loosened on the drum-
heads.
71. *dead*] flavorless.
73. *emblem*] picture expressing a moral fable.

# THE PROLOGUE FOR THE STAGE

For your own sakes, not his, he bade me say,
Would you were come to hear, not see, a play.
Though we his actors must provide for those
Who are our guests here in the way of shows,
The maker hath not so. He'd have you wise     5
Much rather by your ears than by your eyes,
And prays you'll not prejudge his play for ill
Because you mark it not and sit not still,
But have a longing to salute or talk
With such a female and from her to walk     10
With your discourse, to what is done and where,
How, and by whom, in all the town but here.
Alas, what is it to his scene to know
How many coaches in Hyde Park did show
Last spring, what fare today at Medley's was,     15
If Dunstan or the Phoenix best wine has?
They are things— But yet the stage might stand as well
If it did neither hear these things nor tell.
Great noble wits, be good unto yourselves
And make a difference 'twixt poetic elves     20
And poets: All that dabble in the ink
And defile quills are not those few can think,
Conceive, express, and steer the souls of men,
As with a rudder, round thus, with their pen.
He must be one that can instruct your youth     25
And keep your acme in the state of truth,

---

2. *hear, not see*] This distinction between spectators and hearers appeared earlier in *Bartholomew Fair*, Induction, 1. 65.

5. *maker*] Jonson follows the Aristotelian practice of stressing the creative and imitative rather than the prophetic role of the poet (Epilogue, 1. 1, and *Timber*, ll. 2347–48).

15. *Medley's*] a fashionable tavern in Milford Lane where meals were served.

16. *Dunstan*] the Devil Tavern in Fleet Street, where Jonson's *Leges Conviviales* was engraved in marble in the room named Apollo; see II.v.127, note.

16. *Phoenix*] a tavern near the Phoenix playhouse in Drury Lane.

26. *acme*] mature age or period of full growth.

Must enterprise this work. Mark but his ways,
What flight he makes, how new. And then he says,
If that not like you that he sends tonight,
'Tis you have left to judge, not he to write.                    30


## THE PROLOGUE FOR THE COURT

A work not smelling of the lamp, tonight,
   But fitted for your Majesty's disport,
   And writ to the meridian of your court,
We bring, and hope it may produce delight,
The rather being offered as a rite                                5
   To scholars, that can judge and fair report
   The sense they hear above the vulgar sort
Of nutcrackers, that only come for sight.
Wherein, although our title, sir, be *News*,
   We yet adventure here to tell you none,          10
   But show you common follies, and so known
That though they are not truths, th'innocent Muse
   Hath made so like, as fant'sy could them state
Or poetry, without scandal, imitate.

---

29. *like*] please.
30. *left*] ceased.

*Prologue for the Court*] for the performance at Court, Shrove Tuesday,
February 19, 1626. This prologue is in the form of a Sidneyan sonnet
although Drummond reports that Jonson "cursed petrarch" and criti-
cized the sonnet as a Procrustes' bed (*The Conversations with William
Drummond*, ll. 60–63).

8. *nutcrackers*] There are many contemporary references to the
practice of cracking nuts at the playhouses.

# The Staple of News

*Aut prodesse volunt, aut delectare poetae:*
*Aut simul & iucunda, & idonea dicere vitae.*

Horace, in *Ars Poetica*

[I.i]

[*Enter*] Pennyboy Junior [*and*] Leatherleg. *His shoemaker has pull'd on a new pair of boots, and he walks in his gown, waistcoat, and trouses expecting his tailor.*

PENNYBOY JUNIOR.

Gramercy, Leatherleg. Get me the spurrier,
And thou hast fitted me.

LEATHERLEG.                    I'll do't presently.          [*Exit.*]

PENNYBOY JUNIOR.

Look to me, wit, and look to my wit, land.
That is, look on me, and with all thine eyes,
Male, female, yea, hermaphroditic eyes,                              5
And those bring all your helps and perspicils
To see me at best advantage and augment
My form as I come forth; for I do feel
I will be one worth looking after shortly.
Now, by and by, that's shortly.

---

0.1–0.3 *His . . . tailor*] F *prints in*     0.3 *trouses*] F; *Trousers F3.*
*margin to right of ll. 1–10.*

---

0.1–3. *Aut . . . Poetica*] epigraph from the title page, 1631; Horace, *The Art of Poetry*, ll. 333–34, which Jonson translates as "Poets would either profit, or delight,/ Or mixing sweet, and fit, teach life the right."

0.3. *trouses*] close-fitting drawers.

2. *presently*] immediately.

3. *Look . . . land*] parodies the opening line of Donne's "Elegie on Prince Henry": "Looke to mee faith, and look to my faith, God" (F. A. Pottle, "Two Notes on Ben Jonson's *Staple of News*," *Modern Language Notes* 40 [1925]:223–24).

6. *perspicils*] optic glasses, telescopes.

*He draws forth his watch and sets it on the table.*

                       'T strikes! One, two,     10
Three, four, five, six. Enough, enough, dear watch,
Thy pulse hath beat enough. Now sleep and rest;
Would thou couldst make the time to do so too.
I'll wind thee up no more. The hour is come
So long expected! There, there, drop my wardship,    15
                    *He throws off his gown.*
My pupil age and vassalage together.
And Liberty, come throw thyself about me,
In a rich suit, cloak, hat, and band, for now
I'll sue out no man's livery but mine own.
I stand on my own feet, so much a year,    20
Right, round and sound, the lord of mine own ground
And (to rhyme to it) threescore thousand pound!

          *He goes to the door and looks.*

Not come? Not yet? Tailor, thou art a vermin,
Worse than the same thou prosecut'st and prick'st
In subtle seam (Go to, I say no more)    25
Thus to retard my longings, on the day
I do write man, to beat thee. One and twenty
Since the clock struck, complete! And thou wilt feel it,
Thou foolish animal! I could pity him
(An' I were not heartily angry with him now)    30
For this one piece of folly he bears about him,
To dare to tempt the fury of an heir
T'above two thousand a year yet hope his custom.

14. thee] *F;* the *F3.*               25. to] *Gifford;* too *F, F3.*
16. pupil age] *F;* Pupillage *F3.*    28. struck] *F3;* strooke *F.*
19. mine] *F3;* miny *F.*

18. *band*] neckband of a shirt, originally narrow and plain but by
the 1620s wide and elaborate and worn with the ruff referred to at
I.ii.131 (Linthicum, p. 156).
    19. *sue . . . livery*] "institute a suit as heir to obtain possession of
lands which are in the hands of the court of wards" *(OED).*
    24. *prosecut'st*] followest to kill.
    25. *subtle*] fine, narrow.

Well, Master Fashioner, there's some must break—
A head, for this your breaking.

[*Enter* Fashioner.]

Are you come, sir?        35

[I.ii]

FASHIONER.

God give your worship joy.

PENNYBOY JUNIOR.                    What, of your staying?
And leaving me to stalk here in my trouses
Like a tame hernshaw for you?

FASHIONER.                    I but waited
Below, till the clock struck.

PENNYBOY JUNIOR.                    Why, if you had come
Before a quarter, would it so have hurt you        5
In reputation to have waited here?

FASHIONER.

No, but your worship might have pleaded nonage
If you had got 'em on ere I could make
Just affidavit of the time.

PENNYBOY JUNIOR.                    That jest
Has gain'd thy pardon. Thou hadst liv'd condemn'd        10
To thine own hell else, never to have wrought
Stitch more for me or any Pennyboy.
I could have hinder'd thee, but now thou art mine.
For one and twenty years or for three lives,
Choose which thou wilt, I'll make thee a copyholder,        15
And thy first bill unquestion'd. Help me on.

*He says his suit.*

I.ii] *F3;* Act. II. Scene IJ. *F.*        Fashioner, P e n n y b o y Junior,
1.] *preceded in F and F3 by S.D.:*        Thomas Barber, Haberdasher.
                                        6. here] *F;* her *F3.*

---

2. *stalk*] "walk with stiff, high, measured steps, like a long-legged
bird [e.g., heron]" *(OED).*
3. *hernshaw*] heron.
14. *three lives*] a lease or grant "in force during the life of the
longest liver of . . . three . . . specified persons" *(OED).*
15. *copyholder*] one who holds lands "at the will of the lord according to the custom of the manor" *(OED).*
16.1. *says*] tries on.

—13—

FASHIONER.

    Presently, sir. I am bound unto your worship.

PENNYBOY JUNIOR.

    Thou shalt be when I have seal'd thee a lease of my custom.

FASHIONER.

    Your worship's barber is without.

PENNYBOY JUNIOR.               Who? Tom?

    Come in, Tom.

              [*Enter* Thomas Barber.]

              Set thy things upon the board       20

And spread thy cloths. Lay all forth *in procinctu*

And tell's what news.

THOMAS BARBER.         Oh, sir, a staple of news!

    Or the New Staple, which you please.

PENNYBOY JUNIOR.         What's that?

FASHIONER.

    An office, sir, a brave young office set up.

    I had forgot to tell your worship.

PENNYBOY JUNIOR.        For what?      25

THOMAS BARBER.

    To enter all the news, sir, o'the time,

FASHIONER.

    And vent it as occasion serves! A place

Of huge commerce it will be!

PENNYBOY JUNIOR.        Pray thee peace.

    I cannot abide a talking tailor. Let Tom

    (He's a barber) by his place relate it.      30

    What is't, an office, Tom?

THOMAS BARBER.        Newly erected

    Here in the house, almost on the same floor,

    Where all the news of all sorts shall be brought,

---

21. cloths] *Whalley; clothes F;*
*Clothes F3.*

---

    19. *without*] outside.

    21. *in procinctu*] in readiness; since barbers doubled as surgeons, they were expected to know some Latin.

    22. *staple*] market place.

    24. *brave*] fine.

And there be examin'd, and then register'd,
And so be issu'd under the seal of the Office,                    35
As Staple News, no other news be current.

PENNYBOY JUNIOR.

'Fore me, thou speak'st of a brave business, Tom.

FASHIONER.

Nay, if you knew the brain that hatch'd it, sir—

PENNYBOY JUNIOR.

I know thee well enough. Give him a loaf, Tom.
Quiet his mouth. That oven will be venting else.                    40
Proceed.

THOMAS BARBER.    He tells you true, sir. Master Cymbal
Is Master of the Office. He projected it.
He lies here i'the house, and the great rooms
He has taken for the Office and set up
His desks and classes, tables, and his shelves.                    45

FASHIONER.

He's my customer and a wit, sir, too.
But h'has brave wits under him—

THOMAS BARBER.                              Yes, four emissaries.

PENNYBOY JUNIOR.

Emissaries? Stay, there's a fine new word, Tom!
Pray God it signify anything. What are emissaries?

THOMAS BARBER.

Men employ'd outward, that are sent abroad                    50
To fetch in the commodity.

FASHIONER.                              From all regions
Where the best news are made,

THOMAS BARBER.                              Or vented forth,

FASHIONER.

By way of exchange or trade.

35. so be] *F;* so to be *F3.*

---

39. *loaf*] "It was imputed to them [tailors] that they were im-
moderately fond of rolls, hot or cold" (Nares).
40. *venting*] ejecting or discharging, as smoke from an oven.
40. *else*] otherwise.
43. *lies*] lodges.
47. *emissaries*] persons sent out to get information "implying something odious or underhand in the mission, or its manner" *(OED).*

PENNYBOY JUNIOR.                 Nay, thou wilt speak—
FASHIONER.
     My share, sir. There's enough for both.
PENNYBOY JUNIOR.                 Go on then.
     Speak all thou canst. Methinks the ordinaries      55
     Should help them much.
                   *He gives the* Tailor *leave to talk.*
FASHIONER.              Sir, they have ordinaries
     And extraordinaries, as many changes
     And variations as there are points i'the compass.
THOMAS BARBER.
     But the four cardinal quarters—
PENNYBOY JUNIOR.             Ay, those, Tom—
THOMAS BARBER.
     The Court, sir, Paul's, Exchange, and Westminster Hall.    60
PENNYBOY JUNIOR.
     Who is the chief? Which hath precedency?
THOMAS BARBER.
     The governor o'the Staple, Master Cymbal.
     He is the chief, and after him the emissaries.
     First, emissary Court, one Master Fitton.
     He's a jeerer, too.
PENNYBOY JUNIOR.     What's that?
FASHIONER.             A wit.          65
THOMAS BARBER.
     Or half a wit. Some of them are half-wits.
     Two to a wit, there are a set of 'em.
     Then Master Ambler, emissary Paul's,

---

55. *canst*] knowest.

55. *ordinaries*] taverns where meals were available.

60. *Paul's, Exchange*] St. Paul's Cathedral and the Royal Exchange were centers of gossip and newsmongering. H.S. quote from Barnabe Rich, *My Ladies Looking Glasse*, 1606, p. 52: "The News-monger . . . about ten of the clocke in the fore-noone, you may hitte vpon him in the middle walke in *Pauls:* but from aleauen to twelue, hee will not misse the *Exchange*."

60. *Westminster Hall*] housed the Courts of Common Law and Chancery.

68–70. *Ambler . . . Buz*] Although they are alluded to a number of times, neither makes an appearance in the play. The roles of both are given in *Neptune's Triumph*, ll. 295–97, where they were to

A fine-pac'd gentleman as you shall see walk
The middle aisle. And then my froy Hans Buz,          70
A Dutchman; he's emissary Exchange.

FASHIONER.
I had thought Master Burst the merchant had had it.

THOMAS BARBER.                                        No,
He has a rupture; he has sprung a leak.
Emissary Westminster's undispos'd of yet.
Then the Examiner, Register, and two clerks.          75
They manage all at home, and sort and file
And seal the news and issue them.

PENNYBOY JUNIOR.                    Tom, dear Tom,
What may my means do for thee? Ask and have it.
I'd fain be doing some good. It is my birthday,
And I'd do it betimes. I feel a grudging             80
Of bounty, and I would not long lie fallow.
I pray thee think and speak or wish for something.

THOMAS BARBER.
I would I had but one o'the clerks' places
I'this News Office.

PENNYBOY JUNIOR.        Thou shalt have it, Tom,
If silver or gold will fetch it. What's the rate?    85
At what is't set i'the market?

THOMAS BARBER.                    Fifty pound, sir.

PENNYBOY JUNIOR.
An't were a hundred, Tom, thou shalt not want it.

---

71. Exchange] *F3;* Exhange *F.*

---

present meats for the olla podrida: "Graue Mʳ Ambler, Newes-master
of Poules/ Supplies your Capon; and growne Captaine Buz/ (His
Emissary) vnderwrites for Turky." J. B. Williams identifies Hans Buz
as Matthew de Quester, Postmaster of England for Foreign Parts (*A
History of English Journalism,* 1904, p. 22). "The postmasters of
Europe's leading cities had long functioned as the men who collected
the news in their areas and then forwarded it to . . . central trans-
mission points . . . the postmasters were a rudimentary press service"
(Frank, p. 3).
   70. *froy*] handsome, dapper, used ironically (mod. Dutch *fraay*).
   80. *betimes*] speedily.
   80. *grudging*] longing.

FASHIONER.

    Oh, noble master!

        *The* Tailor *leaps and embraceth him.*

PENNYBOY JUNIOR.    How now, Aesop's ass,

    Because I play with Tom must I needs run

    Into your rude embraces? Stand you still, sir.      90

    Clowns' fawnings are a horse's salutations.

    How dost thou like my suit, Tom?

THOMAS BARBER.              Master Fashioner

    Has hit your measures, sir. H'has molded you

    And made you, as they say.

FASHIONER.            No, no, not I,

    I am an ass, old Aesop's ass.

PENNYBOY JUNIOR.         Nay, Fashioner,    95

    I can do thee a good turn too. Be not musty

    Though thou hast molded me, as little Tom says.

    I think thou hast put me in moldy pockets.

                 *He draws out his pockets.*

FASHIONER.                 As good

    Right Spanish perfume, the Lady Estifania's.

    They cost twelve pound a pair.

PENNYBOY JUNIOR.        Thy bill will say so.    100

    I pray thee tell me, Fashioner, what authors

    Thou read'st to help thy invention? Italian prints

    Or arras hangings? They are tailors' libraries.

FASHIONER.

    I scorn such helps.

PENNYBOY JUNIOR.    Oh, though thou art a silkworm

    And deal'st in satins and velvets and rich plushes,    105

    Thou canst not spin all forms out of thyself;

---

    88. *Aesop's ass*] the ass who tried unsuccessfully to gain his master's favor by behaving like the dog.

    96. *musty*] with a pun on *musty* as (1) peevish and (2) moldy.

    99. *Lady Estifania's*] Wittipol mentions as the most important ingredient of the Spanish fucus (cosmetic): "the water/ Of the white Hen of the Lady Estifania's" (*The Devil is an Ass*, IV.iv.39–40).

    103. *arras*] "a rich tapestry fabric, in which figures and scenes are worked in colours" (*OED*).

They are quite other things. I think this suit
Has made me wittier than I was.

FASHIONER.                              Believe it, sir,
That clothes do much upon the wit as weather
Does on the brain, and thence comes your proverb:      110
The tailor makes the man. I speak by experience
Of my own customers. I have had gallants,
Both court and country, would ha' fool'd you up
In a new suit, with the best wits in being,
And kept their speed as long as their clothes lasted      115
Han'some and neat; but then as they grew out
At the elbows again or had a stain or spot,
They have sunk most wretchedly.

PENNYBOY JUNIOR.                        What thou report'st
Is but the common calamity and seen daily,
And therefore you have another answering proverb:      120
A broken sleeve keeps the arm back.

FASHIONER.                              'Tis true, sir,
And thence we say that such a one plays at peep-arm.

PENNYBOY JUNIOR.
Do you so? It is wittily said. I wonder, gentlemen
And men of means will not maintain themselves
Fresher in wit, I mean in clothes, to the highest.      125
For he that's out o' clothes is out o' fashion,
And out of fashion is out of countenance,
And out o' countenance is out o' wit.
Is not rogue Haberdasher come?

[*Enter* Haberdasher, Linener, *and* Leatherleg.] *They are all about him, busy.*

HABERDASHER.                            Yes, here, sir.
I ha' been without this half hour.

116. Han'some] *F;* Handsom *F3.*     120. you have] *F;* you'ave *F3.*

---

111. *The tailor . . . man*] proverb (Tilley, T 17).
113. *fool'd you up*] fooled you completely.
115. *speed*] prosperity, good fortune.
121. *A broken sleeve . . . back*] proverb (Tilley, S 53).

PENNYBOY JUNIOR.                                    Give me my hat.          130
    Put on my girdle. Rascal, sits my ruff well?
LINENER.
    In print.
PENNYBOY JUNIOR.    Slave.
LINENER.                          See yourself.
PENNYBOY JUNIOR.                                Is this same hat
    O'the block passant? Do not answer me.
    I cannot stay for an answer. I do feel
    The powers of one and twenty, like a tide,          135
    Flow in upon me, and perceive an heir
    Can conjure up all spirits in all circles.
    Rogue, rascal, slave, give tradesmen their true names
    And they appear to 'em presently.
LINENER [aside]                              For profit.
PENNYBOY JUNIOR.
    Come, cast my cloak about me. I'll go see          140
    This Office, Tom, and be trimm'd afterwards.
    I'll put thee in possession, my prime work!

                    *His Spurrier comes in.*

    Godso, my spurrier. Put 'em on, boy, quickly.
    I had like to ha' lost my spurs with too much speed.


[I.iii]
[*Enter*] Pennyboy Canter [*in a patched and ragged cloak*], *to
them, singing.*

PENNYBOY CANTER.

    *Good morning to my joy, my jolly Pennyboy,
        The lord and the prince of plenty!*

133. not answer] *F;* not not answer *F3.*

---

[I.ii]
    132. *In print*] in a precise and perfect way.
    133. *passant*] current.
    139. *appear to 'em*] respond to their names.
    143. *Godso*] an expletive based on catso, from Ital. *cazzo*, penis.
    144. *lost . . . spurs*] one part of the ceremony of degradation; others
are mentioned at IV.Intermean 57–58.

> I come to see what riches thou bearest in thy breeches,
>   The first of thy one and twenty.
> What, do thy pockets jingle? Or shall we need to mingle        5
>   Our strength both of foot and horses?
> These fellows look so eager, as if they would beleaguer
>   An heir in the midst of his forces!
> I hope they be no sergeants that hang upon thy margents.
>   This rogue has the jowl of a jailor!                         10

> The young Pennyboy answers in tune.

PENNYBOY JUNIOR.

> Oh Founder, no such matter. My spurrier and my hatter.
>   My linen-man and my tailor.
> Thou shouldst have been brought in too, shoemaker,
> If the time had been longer, and Tom Barber.
> How dost thou like my company, old Canter?                     15
> Do I not muster a brave troupe, all bill men?
> Present your arms before my Founder here.
> This is my Founder, this same learned Canter.
> He brought me the first news of my father's death,
> I thank him, and ever since, I call him Founder.               20
> Worship him, boys. I'll read only the sums
> And pass 'em straight.

> He takes the bills and puts them up in his pockets.

LEATHERLEG.                    Now ale—

FASHIONER. LINENER. HABERDASHER. SPURRIER. BARBER.

>                    —And strong ale bless him.

22. S.P.s FASHIONER . . . BARBER]
this edn.; Rest F, F3.

---

9. *sergeants*] sheriff's officers who arrested gentlemen for unpaid debts.

9. *margents*] flanks.

16. *bill men*] with a pun on (1) soldiers or watchmen armed with "bills," and (2) tradesmen who present "bills."

21. *Worship*] salute.

22. *straight*] at once.

PENNYBOY JUNIOR.

    Godso, some ale and sugar for my Founder!

    Good bills, sufficient bills, these bills may pass.

PENNYBOY CANTER.

    I do not like those paper-squibs, good master.     25

    They may undo your store, I mean of credit,

    And fire your arsenal if case you do not

    In time make good those outer-works, your pockets,

    And take a garrison in of some two hundred,

    To beat these pioneers off, that carry a mine     30

    Would blow you up at last. Secure your casamates.

    Here, Master Picklock, sir, your man o' law

    And learn'd attorney, has sent you a bag of munition.

PENNYBOY JUNIOR [*takes the bag*].

    What is't?

PENNYBOY CANTER.    Three hundred pieces.

PENNYBOY JUNIOR.               I'll dispatch 'em.

PENNYBOY CANTER.

    Do, I would have your strengths lin'd and perfum'd,    35

    With gold as well as amber.

PENNYBOY JUNIOR.          God-a-mercy,

    Come *ad solvendum*, boys!         *He pays all.*

                There, there, and there, &c.

    I look on nothing but *totalis*.

PENNYBOY CANTER [*aside*].     See

    The difference 'twixt the covetous and the prodigal!

34. S.D.] *Gifford*.

---

   23. *sugar*] commonly used to sweeten ale and wine.

   24. *sufficient bills*] bills in their proper form.

   27. *if case*] perchance.

   30. *pioneers*] foot-soldiers who dig trenches and lay mines.

   31. *casamates*] positions under a wall or bulwark from which the enemy can be shot as he enters the ditch to try to scale the wall.

   36. *amber*] ambergris.

   36. *God-a-mercy*] God have mercy, i.e., God reward you.

   37. *ad solvendum*] now for paying.

   38. *totalis*] Dekker recommends that the gallant paying a tavern reckoning cast his "eie onely vpon the *Totalis* and no further," so no one would think he knew the current prices of individual items or worse still that he was paterfamilias (*The Guls Horne-book*, Chap. 7).

"The covetous man never has money, and                    40
The prodigal will have none shortly."
PENNYBOY JUNIOR.                              Ha,
What says my Founder? —I thank you, I thank you, sirs.
LEATHERLEG. FASHIONER. LINENER. HABERDASHER. SPURRIER. BARBER.
God bless your worship and your worship's Chanter.

  [*Exeunt* Leatherleg, Fashioner, Linener, *and* Haberdasher.]

PENNYBOY CANTER.
I say 'tis nobly done to cherish shopkeepers
And pay their bills without examining, thus.                    45
PENNYBOY JUNIOR.
Alas, they have had a pitiful hard time on't,
A long vacation from their cozening.
Poor rascals, I do do it out of charity.
I would advance their trade again and have them
Haste to be rich, swear and forswear wealthily.                    50
  [*To the* Spurrier.]   What do you stay for, sirrah?
SPURRIER.                              To my box, sir.
PENNYBOY JUNIOR *(he gives the* Spurrier *to his box).*
Your box, why, there's an angel. If my spurs
Be not right Ripon—
SPURRIER.                    Give me never a penny
If I strike not through your bounty with the rowels.   [*Exit.*]
PENNYBOY JUNIOR.
Dost thou want any money, Founder?
PENNYBOY CANTER.                    Who, sir, I?                    55

43. S.P.] *this edn.;* All *F, F3*

---

40–41. *"The covetous . . . shortly."*] translation of Seneca *De
Remediis Fortuitorum* 10.3 (H.S.).
  43. *Chanter*] singer; one of the many changes Jonson rings upon
Pennyboy Canter's name.
  47. *cozening*] cheating.
  52. S.D. *gives . . . to his box*] i.e., drops a coin in the Spurrier's box.
  52. *angel*] a coin worth about ten shillings.
  53. *Ripon*] "a [Yorkshire] Town famous for the best spurs of *England,* whose *rowels* may be enforced to strike through a shilling"
(Nares).

Did I not tell you I was bred i'the mines
Under Sir Bevis Bullion?

PENNYBOY JUNIOR.                         That is true,
I quite forgot. You mine men want no money;
Your streets are pav'd with't. There, the molten silver
Runs out like cream on cakes of gold.

PENNYBOY CANTER.                         And rubies          60
Do grow like strawberries.

PENNYBOY JUNIOR.               'Twere brave being there.
Come, Tom, we'll go to the Office now.

PENNYBOY CANTER.                         What office?

PENNYBOY JUNIOR.

News Office, the New Staple. Thou shalt go too.
'Tis here i'the house, on the same floor, Tom says.
Come, Founder, let us trade in ale and nutmegs. [*Exeunt.*] 65

[I.iv]

[*Enter*] Register [*and* Nathaniel *together and*] a Countrywoman
[*who*] *waits there.*

REGISTER.

What, are those desks fit now? Set forth the table,
The carpet, and the chair. Where are the news
That were examin'd last? Ha' you fil'd them up?

NATHANIEL.

Not yet, I had no time.

0.1–0.2.] Register, Clerk, Woman.     4. S.P. NATHANIEL] *Gifford;* Cle.
*F, F3. F prints in margin to right     throughout this scene in F, F3.*
*of ll. 11–12: "A countrey-woman*
*waites there."*

---

57. *Sir Bevis Bullion*] Sir Bevis Bulmer, famous mining engineer and
speculator, was knighted in 1604; he became very wealthy as a result
of his speculations but died in debt in 1615. He was apparently a
generous employer and philanthropist (Knights, pp. 89–94).
65. *trade in*] drive a trade in.
65. *ale and nutmegs*] Nutmeg, like many spices, was used to flavor
ale; since nutmeg is reputed to be an intoxicant, the combination
was probably more potent than ale alone.
[I.iv]
2. *carpet*] a woolen tablecloth.

REGISTER.                    Are those news register'd
That emissary Buz sent in last night                    5
Of Spinola and his eggs?
NATHANIEL.                    Yes sir, and fil'd.
REGISTER.
What are you now upon?
NATHANIEL.                    That our new emissary
Westminster gave us of the Golden Heir.
REGISTER.
Dispatch. That's news, indeed, and of importance.

[*To the* Countrywoman.]

What would you have, good woman?
WOMAN.                    I would have, sir,    10
A groatsworth of any news, I care not what,
To carry down this Saturday to our vicar.
REGISTER.
Oh, you are a butterwoman. Ask Nathaniel,
The clerk there.
NATHANIEL.          Sir, I tell her she must stay
Till emissary Exchange or Paul's send in,                    15
And then I'll fit her.
REGISTER.                    Do, good woman, have patience.
It is not now as when the Captain liv'd.

[*Exit* Woman.]

---

6. *Spinola*] Ambrogio di Spinola, an Italian who served as a general
for Spain before and during the Thirty Years War. He conquered
the Palatinate in 1620, driving out James I's son-in-law Frederick. One
of his most famous victories, the capture of Breda after a ten-month
seige, took place on June 5, 1625, less than a year before *The Staple*
was acted.

6. *eggs*] Details of the eggs are given at III.ii.46–52.

11. *groatsworth*] as much as a fourpenny coin will buy.

13. *butterwoman . . . Nathaniel*] The first of many punning allusions to the stationer Nathaniel Butter.

14. *stay*] wait.

16. *fit*] supply.

17.] one of many contemporary echoes of *The Spanish Tragedy*,
III.xiv.111: "It is not now as when Andrea liu'd." There are frequent
references in contemporary plays to this captain, Thomas Gainsford,
an associate of Nathaniel Butter's (Frank, pp. 9–13).

NATHANIEL.

    You'll blast the reputation of the Office,
    Now i'the bud, if you dispatch these groats
    So soon. Let them attend in name of policy.        20

[I.v]

      [*Enter to them*] Pennyboy Junior, Cymbal, Fitton.

PENNYBOY JUNIOR.

    In troth, they are dainty rooms. What place is this?
CYMBAL.

    This is the outer room, where my clerks sit
    And keep their sides; the Register i'th midst,
    The Examiner, he sits private there, within,
    And here I have my several rolls and files        5
    Of news by the alphabet, and all put up
    Under their heads.
PENNYBOY JUNIOR.      But those, too, subdivided?
CYMBAL.

    Into authentical and apocryphal—
FITTON.

    Or news of doubtful credit: as barbers' news—
CYMBAL.

    And tailors' news, porters' and watermen's news.    10
FITTON.

    Whereto, beside the *coranti* and *gazetti*—
CYMBAL.

    I have the news of the season—
FITTON.                     As vacation news,
    Term news, and Christmas news.

0.1] Pennyboy Junior, Cymbal,
Fitton, Thomas Barber, Canter.
*F, F3.*

---

    19. *groats*] with a pun on *groats* as (1) fourpenny coins and (2)
hulled oats.
    20. *attend*] wait, tarry.

[I.v]
    11. *coranti and gazetti*] single-sheet compilations of news.
    12–13. *vacation . . . Term*] with reference to the periods of the

CYMBAL.                        And news o'the faction—
FITTON.

As the Reformed news, Protestant news.
CYMBAL.

And Pontificial news, of all which several,                    15
The day-books, characters, precedents are kept,
Together with the names of special friends—
FITTON.

And men of correspondence i'the country—
CYMBAL.

Yes, of all ranks and all religions—
FITTON.

Factors and agents—
CYMBAL.                        Liegers, that lie out                    20
Through all the shires o'the kingdom.
PENNYBOY JUNIOR.                        This is fine
And bears a brave relation! But what says
*Mercurius Britannicus* to this?
CYMBAL.

Oh sir, he gains by't half in half.
FITTON.                        Nay, more,
I'll stand to't. For, where he was wont to get                    25
In hungry captains, obscure statesmen—
CYMBAL.                        Fellows
To drink with him in a dark room in a tavern
And eat a sausage—
FITTON.                        We ha' seen't.

---

year when the law courts were adjourned, and the terms when they
were in session.
  14–21. *As  . . . kingdom*] Many phrases in these lines appeared
earlier in the Factor's speech (*News from the New World,* ll. 33–43).
  15. *Pontificial*] pontifical, papist.
  20. *Liegers*] resident agents.
  23. *Mercurius Britannicus*] For two and a half years, beginning December, 1624, a series of newsbooks was issued under this imprint by
Nathaniel Butter and Nicholas Bourne.
  24. *half in half*] by half the total amount.

CYMBAL.                                    As fain
   To keep so many politic pens
   Going to feed the press—
FITTON.                      And dish out news,                    30
   Were't true or false—
CYMBAL.                  Now all that charge is sav'd.
   The public chronicler—
FITTON.                      How do you call him there?
CYMBAL.
   And gentle reader—
FITTON.                  He that has the maidenhead
   Of all the books—
CYMBAL.                  Yes, dedicated to him—
FITTON.
   Or rather prostituted—
PENNYBOY JUNIOR.            You are right, sir.                    35
CYMBAL.
   —No more shall be abus'd, nor country parsons
   O'the inquisition, nor busy justices
   Trouble the peace, and both torment themselves
   And their poor ign'rant neighbors with inquiries
   After the many and most innocent monsters,               40
   That never came i'th' counties they were charg'd with.
PENNYBOY JUNIOR.
   Why, methinks, sir, if the honest common people
   Will be abus'd, why should not they ha' their pleasure
   In the believing lies are made for them,
   As you i'th' Office, making them yourselves?              45

29. politic] *H.S. query* politician.    41. they] *F;* the *F3.*

---

28. *fain*] obliged.
29. *politic pens*] cunning writers.
32. *How . . . there?*] H.S. retain the comma after "How" and
suggest a reference to Edmund Howes, who continued Stow's *Chronicle.*
40–41. *many . . . with*] like the serpent of Sussex, to whom the
Factor refers (*News from the New World,* ll. 48–51).
42–45. *Why . . . yourselves*] This speech is almost verbatim the
question the Printer puts to the Factor (*News from the New World,*
ll. 52–55).

FITTON.

    Oh sir, it is the printing we oppose.

CYMBAL.

    We not forbid that any news be made
    But that't be printed, for when news is printed,
    It leaves, sir, to be news. While 'tis but written—

FITTON.

    Though it be ne'er so false, it runs news still.       50

PENNYBOY JUNIOR.

    See divers men's opinions! Unto some,
    The very printing of them makes them news,
    That ha' not the heart to believe anything
    But what they see in print.

FITTON.                    Ay, that's an error

    Has abus'd many; but we shall reform it,       55
    As many things beside (we have a hope)
    Are crept among the popular abuses.

CYMBAL.

    Nor shall the stationer cheat upon the time,
    By buttering over again—

FITTON.                Once in seven years,

    As the age dotes—

CYMBAL.         And grows forgetful o'them,      60

    His antiquated pamphlets, with new dates.
    But all shall come from the mint—

FITTON.                  Fresh and new stamp'd—

CYMBAL.

    With the Office seal, Staple commodity.

FITTON.

    And if a man will assure his news, he may.
    Twopence a sheet he shall be warranted      65
    And have a policy for't.

---

    46–50. *Oh . . . still*] These lines repeat the Factor's distinction (*News from the New World*, ll. 57–60).

    51–54. *See . . . print*] Again Pennyboy Junior echoes the Printer's explanation (*News from the New World*, ll. 61–63).

    51. *divers*] diverse.

    58–61. *Nor . . . dates*] This is the very practice to which the Printer confesses (*News from the New World*, ll. 65–67).

    58. *stationer*] a publishing bookseller.

PENNYBOY JUNIOR.          Sir, I admire
   The method o' your place. All things within't
   Are so digested, fitted, and compos'd,
   As it shows Wit had married Order.
FITTON.                                        Sir—
CYMBAL.
   The best we could to invite the times.
FITTON.                              It has                       70
   Cost sweat and freezing.
CYMBAL.                    And some broken sleeps
   Before it came to this.
PENNYBOY JUNIOR.          I easily think it.
FITTON.
   But now it has the shape—
CYMBAL.                    And is come forth.
PENNYBOY JUNIOR.
   A most polite neat thing! With all the limbs
   As sense can taste!
CYMBAL.              It is, sir, though I say it,              75
   As well-begotten a business and as fairly
   Help'd to the world.
PENNYBOY JUNIOR.        You must be a midwife, sir.
   Or else the son of a midwife (pray you pardon me)
   Have help'd it forth so happily! What news ha' you?
   News o' this morning? I would fain hear some         80
   Fresh from the forge (as new as day, as they say).
CYMBAL.
   And such we have, sir.
REGISTER.              Show him the last roll,
   Of emissary Westminster's, "The Heir."
PENNYBOY JUNIOR.
   Come nearer, Tom.

---

   69. *Wit . . . Order*] after the manner of such old-fashioned play
titles as *The Marriage of Wit and Science* (ca. 1569) and *The Marriage
of Wit and Wisdom* (ca. 1579).
   74. *polite*] orderly.
   75. *taste*] experience.
   81. *as new as day*] a phrase Latimer characterizes as appropriate
to a fishwife (*The New Inn*, IV.iii.31).

[*Enter* Thomas Barber.]

NATHANIEL.                    There is a brave young heir
Is come of age this morning, Master Pennyboy.
                            Pennyboy *rejoiceth that he is in.*
PENNYBOY JUNIOR.                              That's I.   85
NATHANIEL.
His father died on this day seventh-night.
PENNYBOY JUNIOR.                        True.
NATHANIEL.
At six o' the clock i'the morning, just a week
Ere he was one and twenty.
PENNYBOY JUNIOR.            I am here, Tom!
Proceed, I pray thee.
NATHANIEL.            An old canting beggar
Brought him first news, whom he has entertain'd          90
To follow him since.
PENNYBOY JUNIOR.        Why, you shall see him. —Founder,
Come in;

                    *Calls in the* Canter.

        No follower but companion.
I pray thee put him in, friend. There's an angel—
                        *He gives the* Clerk [*a coin*].
Thou dost not know, he's a wise old fellow
Though he seem patch'd thus and made up o' pieces.    95
                            [*Exit* Nathaniel.]
Founder, we are in, here, in, i'the News Office!
In this day's roll, already! I do muse
How you came by us, sirs.

84. S.P. NATHANIEL] *Gifford;* Cla.      88–89.] F *prints in margin:* "Tels
*throughout this scene in F, F3.*        Thom: *of it.*"
86. seventh-] *F;* seven- *F3.*          92. S.D. Calls] *F3; Call F.*
                                         95.1.] *Gifford.*

86. *seventh-*] This use of an ordinal for a cardinal is the single
instance of this error in Jonson and probably a printer's error
(Partridge, p. 120).
90. *entertain'd*] kept in his service.

CYMBAL.                                    One Master Picklock,
    A lawyer, that hath purchas'd here a place,
    This morning, of an emissary under me—                    100
FITTON.
    Emissary Westminster.
CYMBAL.                              Gave it into th'Office—
FITTON.
    For his essay, his piece.
PENNYBOY JUNIOR.              My man o' law!
    He's my attorney and solicitor, too!
    A fine pragmatic! What's his place worth?
CYMBAL.
    A *nemo-scit,* sir.
FITTON.                        'Tis as news come in—                   105
CYMBAL.
    —And as they are issued. I have the just moiety
    For my part. Then the other moiety
    Is parted into seven. The four emissaries,
    Whereof my cousin Fitton here's for Court,
    Ambler for Paul's, and Buz for the Exchange,            110
    Picklock for Westminster, with the Examiner
    And Register, they have full parts. And then one part
    Is underparted to a couple of clerks,
    And there's the just division of the profits.
PENNYBOY JUNIOR.
    Ha' you those clerks, sir?
CYMBAL.                                  There is one desk empty,       115
    But it has many suitors.
PENNYBOY JUNIOR.              Sir, may I
    Present one more and carry it if his parts
    Or gifts (which you will, call 'em)—
CYMBAL.                                  Be sufficient, sir.

---

    104. *pragmatic*] man of business.
    105. *nemo-scit*] no one knows.
    106. *moiety*] half.
    113. *underparted*] subdivided.
    117. *carry it*] win the contest.
    117. *parts*] abilities.

PENNYBOY JUNIOR.

    What are your present clerk's abilities?

    How is he qualified?

CYMBAL.               A decay'd stationer                    120

    He was, but knows news well, can sort and rank 'em.

FITTON.

    And for a need can make 'em.

CYMBAL.                True Paul's bred,

    I'the Churchyard.

PENNYBOY JUNIOR.    And this at the West door,

    O'th' other side. He's my barber, Tom,

    A pretty scholar and a Master of Arts,                    125

    Was made, or went out Master of Arts in a throng,

    At the University; as before, one Christmas,

    He got into a masque at court, by his wit

    And the good means of his cittern, holding up thus

    For one o'the music. He's a nimble fellow                    130

    And alike skill'd in every liberal science,

    As having certain snaps of all, a neat

    Quick vein in forging news, too. I do love him,

    And promis'd him a good turn, and I would do it.

    What's your price? The value?

CYMBAL.                Fifty pounds, sir.                    135

PENNYBOY JUNIOR.

    Get in, Tom. Take possession, I install thee.

---

123. *Churchyard*] where many of the stationers' shops were located.

123. *West door*] where advertisements for servingmen seeking employment were posted.

125–26. *Master of Arts . . . throng*] When King James visited Oxford in 1605 and Cambridge in 1615, degrees were conferred on his retinue. John Nichols quotes from an account of St. John's College, Cambridge: "Degrees were vilely prostituted to mean persons, such as apothecaries and barbers." Among those who received such degrees but were later degraded was one Walterus Priest, *tonsor* (*The Progresses, Processions, and Magnificent Festivities of King James the First* [1828], vol. 3, p. 61).

129. *cittern*] lutelike instrument available for customers to play while they waited at barbershops.

132. *snaps*] fragments, scraps; there is a pun on the practice (often alluded to in Jacobean drama) of barbers snapping their fingers as they go about their work.

Here, tell your money. Give thee joy, good Tom,
And let me hear from thee every minute of news,
While the New Staple stands or the Office lasts,
Which I do wish may ne'er be less, for thy sake.     140

[*Re-enter* Nathaniel.]

NATHANIEL [*to* Cymbal].
     The emissaries, sir, would speak with you
And Master Fitton. They have brought in news,
Three bale together.
CYMBAL [*to* Pennyboy Junior].   Sir, you are welcome here.
FITTON.
     So is your creature.
CYMBAL.                Business calls us off, sir,
That may concern the Office.
PENNYBOY JUNIOR.                Keep me fair, sir,     145
Still i'your Staple. I am here your friend,
On the same floor.
FITTON.                We shall be your servants.

*They* [Cymbal, Fitton, *and* Register] *take leave of* Pennyboy
[Junior] *and* [Pennyboy] Canter.
PENNYBOY JUNIOR.
     How dost thou like it, Founder?
PENNYBOY CANTER.                All is well,
But that your man o' law, methinks, appears not
In his due time. Oh, here comes master's worship.     150

[I.vi]                [*Enter*] Picklock.

PICKLOCK.
     How does the heir, bright Master Pennyboy?
Is he awake yet in his one and twenty?
Why, this is better far than to wear cypress,

137–39.] *F prints in margin: "Hee*     [I.vi]
*buyes* Thom *a* Clerkes place."     0.1.] Picklock, Pennyboy Junior,
                                   Pennyboy Canter. *F, F3*.

137. *tell*] count.
[I.vi]
     3. *cypress*] black fabric used as a symbol of mourning.

Dull smutting gloves or melancholy blacks,
And have a pair of twelvepenny broad ribbons                    5
Laid out like labels.

PENNYBOY JUNIOR.          I should ha' made shift
To have laugh'd as heartily in my mourner's hood
As in this suit if it had pleas'd my father
To have been buried with the trumpeters.

PICKLOCK.
The Heralds of Arms, you mean.

PENNYBOY JUNIOR.                    I mean                    10
All noise that is superfluous.

PICKLOCK.                         All that idle pomp
And vanity of a tombstone, your wise father
Did, by his will, prevent. Your worship had—

PENNYBOY JUNIOR.
A loving and obedient father of him,
I know it, a right, kind-natur'd man                    15
To die so opportunely.

PICKLOCK.                    And to settle
All things so well, compounded for your wardship
The week afore, and left your state entire
Without any charge upon't.

PENNYBOY JUNIOR.               I must needs say,
I lost an officer of him, a good bailiff,                    20
And I shall want him. But all peace be with him.
I will not wish him alive again, not I,
For all my fortune. Give your worship joy
O' your new place, your emissaryship
I'the News Office.

PICKLOCK.               Know you why I bought it, sir?                    25

PENNYBOY JUNIOR.
Not I.

---

4. *smutting*] making gloomy.
5. *twelvepenny broad ribbons*] the widest ribbon available; the English penny was a standard measure of ribbon width (Linthicum, p. 283).
6. *like labels*] hanging down from the sides of his hat.
6. *made shift*] managed successfully.
20. *bailiff*] manager, steward.

PICKLOCK.   To work for you and carry a mine
    Against the master of it, Master Cymbal,
    Who hath a plot upon a gentlewoman
    Was once design'd for you, sir.
PENNYBOY JUNIOR.          Me?
PICKLOCK.                Your father,
    Old Master Pennyboy, of happy memory,        30
    And wisdom too, as any i'the county,
    Careful to find out a fit match for you
    In his own lifetime (but he was prevented),
    Left it in writing in a schedule here,
    To be annexed to his will, that you,        35
    His only son, upon his charge and blessing,
    Should take due notice of a gentlewoman
    Sojourning with your uncle, Richer Pennyboy.
PENNYBOY JUNIOR.
    A Cornish gentlewoman, I do know her,
    Mistress Pecunia Do-all.
PICKLOCK.             A great lady,      40
    Indeed, she is, and not of mortal race,
    Infanta of the Mines; her Grace's grandfather
    Was Duke, and cousin to the King of Ophir,
    The Subterranean. Let that pass. Her name is,
    Or rather her three names are (for such she is)    45
    Aurelia Clara Pecunia, a great Princess
    Of mighty power though she live in private
    With a contracted family! Her secretary—
PENNYBOY CANTER.
    Who is her gentleman-usher too—
PICKLOCK.             One Broker,
    And then two gentlewomen, Mistress Statute    50
    And Mistress Band, with Wax, the chambermaid,

---

34. *schedule*] codicil.
   39. *Cornish*] As Infanta of the Mines (see l. 42), she reigns over the
mines of Cornwall. William Camden in *Britannia* (trans. Holland,
ed. 1610, p. 186) says of Cornwall: "And not only tin is here found,
but therwith also gold and siluer."
   43. *Ophir*] At Ophir, Solomon used the philosopher's stone to
transmute base metals into gold.
   48. *family*] household.

And Mother Mortgage, the old nurse, two grooms,
Pawn and his fellow. You have not many to bribe, sir.
The work is feasible and th'approaches easy,
By your own kindred. Now, sir, Cymbal thinks,                55
The Master here and governor o'the Staple,
By his fine arts and pomp of his great place
To draw her. He concludes, she is a woman,
And that so soon as sh'hears of the new Office,
She'll come to visit it as they all have longings          60
After new sights and motions. But your bounty,
Person, and bravery must achieve her.

PENNYBOY CANTER.                              She is
The talk o'the time, th'adventure o'the age!

PICKLOCK.
You cannot put yourself upon an action
Of more importance.

PENNYBOY CANTER.        All the world are suitors to her.    65

PICKLOCK.
All sorts of men and all professions!

PENNYBOY CANTER.
You shall have stall-fed doctors, cramm'd divines,
Make love to her, and with those studied
And perfum'd flatteries as no room can stink
More elegant than where they are.

PICKLOCK.                                Well chanted,       70
Old Canter, thou sing'st true.

PENNYBOY CANTER.                  And (by your leave)
Good master's worship, some of your velvet coat
Make corpulent curtsies to her till they crack for't.

PICKLOCK.
There's Doctor Almanac wooes her, one of the jeerers,
A fine physician.

PENNYBOY CANTER.    Your sea captain, Shunfield,            75
Gives out he'll go upon the cannon for her—

PICKLOCK.
Though his loud mouthing get him little credit.

---

61. *motions*] shows.

PENNYBOY CANTER.

    Young Master Piedmantle, the fine herald,
    Professes to derive her through all ages,
    From all the kings and queens that ever were.     80

PICKLOCK.

    And Master Madrigal, the crowned poet
    Of these our times, doth offer at her praises
    As fair as any, when it shall please Apollo
    That wit and rhyme may meet both in one subject.

PENNYBOY CANTER.

    And you to bear her from all these, it will be—     85

PICKLOCK.

    A work of fame—

PENNYBOY CANTER.     Of honor—

PICKLOCK.                 Celebration—

PENNYBOY CANTER.

    Worthy your name.

PICKLOCK.          The Pennyboys to live in't.

PENNYBOY CANTER.

    It is an action you were built for, sir,

PICKLOCK.

    And none but you can do it.

PENNYBOY JUNIOR.        I'll undertake it,

PENNYBOY CANTER.

    And carry it.

PENNYBOY JUNIOR.   Fear me not, for since I came     90
    Of mature age, I have had a certain itch
    In my right eye, this corner here, do you see?
    To do some work, and worthy of a Chronicle.     [*Exeunt.*]

## THE FIRST INTERMEAN AFTER THE FIRST ACT

MIRTH.

    How now, gossip! How does the play please you?

CENSURE.

    Very scurvily, methinks, and sufficiently naught—

79. derive] *F3;* deriuer *F.*

---

    84. *wit*] judgment, intelligence (?).
    0.1. *Intermean*] interlude.

EXPECTATION.

—As a body would wish. Here's nothing but a young
prodigal come of age, who makes much of the barber,
buys him a place in a new Office, i'the air, I know not          5
where, and his man o' law to follow him, with the beggar
to boot, and they two help him to a wife.

MIRTH.

Ay, she is a proper piece that such creatures can broke
for!

TATTLE.

I cannot abide that nasty fellow, the beggar. If he had          10
been a court-beggar in good clothes, a beggar in velvet,
as they say, I could have endur'd him.

MIRTH.

Or a begging scholar in black, or one of these beggarly
poets, gossip, that would hang upon a young heir like
a horseleech.                                                    15

EXPECTATION.

Or a threadbare doctor of physic, a poor quacksalver.

CENSURE.

Or a sea captain, half starv'd.

MIRTH.

Ay, these were tolerable beggars, beggars of fashion!
You shall see some such anon.

TATTLE.

I would fain see the fool, gossip. The fool is the finest          20
man i'the company, they say, and has all the wit. He is
the very justice o' peace o'the play, and can commit
whom he will and what he will—error, absurdity, as the
toy takes him—and no man say black is his eye, but
laugh at him.                                                    25

MIRTH.

But they ha' no fool i'this play, I am afraid, gossip.

22. commit] *F3;* cemmit *F.*

---

19. *anon*] right away, soon.
24. *no man . . . eye*] proverb: "You cannot say black is his eye"
(Tilley, E 252); "that is you can find no fault in him, charge him
with no crime" (Ray).

TATTLE.

It's a wise play then.

EXPECTATION.

They are all fools the rather in that.

CENSURE.

Like enough.

TATTLE.

My husband (Timothy Tattle, God rest his poor soul) 30
was wont to say there was no play without a fool and a
devil in't; he was for the devil still, God bless him.
The devil for his money, would he say. "I would fain
see the devil." "And why would you so fain see the
devil?" would I say. "Because he has horns, wife, and 35
may be a cuckold as well as a devil," he would answer.
"You are e'en such another, husband," quoth I. "Was
the devil ever married? Where do you read the devil
was ever so honorable to commit matrimony?" "The play
will tell us that," says he. "We'll go see't tomorrow, *The* 40
*Devil is an Ass.* He is an arrant learn'd man that made
it, and can write, they say, and I am foully deceiv'd but
he can read too."

MIRTH.

I remember it, gossip, I went with you. By the same
token, Mistress Trouble Truth dissuaded us and told us 45
he was a profane poet and all his plays had devils in
them, that he kept school upo'the stage, could conjure
there, above the School of Westminster and Doctor Lamb
too. Not a play he made but had a devil in it. And that

37–38. *Was . . . married?*] "The devil and his dam" are a proverbial
pair (Tilley, D 225).

40–41. *The Devil is an Ass*] proverbial expression (Tilley, D 242)
as well as the title of Jonson's play.

43. *he can read too*] In 1598 Jonson's ability to read saved his life
when he escaped hanging for killing one of the actors in Henslowe's
company, Gabriel Spencer, by claiming right or benefit of clergy.

45. *dissuaded us*] exhorted us not to go.

48. *School of Westminster*] This allusion is explained in III.Inter-
mean.43–51.

48. *Doctor Lamb*] an astrologer imprisoned for magic practices.
From 1608 to 1623, he was in King's Bench prison in London and
was allowed to receive his many clients there.

he would learn us all to make our husbands cuckolds at  50
plays. By another token, that a young married wife
i'the company said she could find in her heart to steal
thither and see a little o'the vanity through her mask,
and come practice at home.

TATTLE.

Oh, it was Mistress—                                        55

MIRTH.

Nay, gossip, I name nobody. It may be 'twas myself.

EXPECTATION.

But was the devil a proper man, gossip?

MIRTH.

As fine a gentleman of his inches as ever I saw trusted
to the stage, or anywhere else, and lov'd the commonwealth as well as e'er a patriot of 'em all. He would    60
carry away the Vice on his back quick to hell in every
play where he came, and reform abuses.

EXPECTATION.

There was the Devil of Edmonton, no such man, I warrant you.

CENSURE.

The conjurer cozen'd him with a candle's end. He was    65
an ass.

---

58. gentleman . . . inches] "notable fellow" (OED).

60. patriot] pejorative name for a shifting group of members of
Parliament who were critics or opponents of the Crown and active
champions of liberties. "The great 'patriot' names in the house of
the 1620's are those of Sir Edward Coke, Sir Robert Phelips, Sir John
Eliot, and John Pym" (William M. Mitchell, The Rise of the Revolu-
tionary Party in the House of Commons, 1603–1629 [New York, 1957],
p. 51). See V.vi.46–48, note.

63. Devil of Edmonton] The anonymous comedy The Merry Devil
of Edmonton, 1602, was so popular that a third edition was published
in 1626.

65. conjurer . . . candle's end] In the extant version of the play
of The Merry Devil, the conjurer, Peter Fabel, does not use this trick.
It does appear, however, in a prose tract entitled The Life and Death
of the Merry Devill of Edmonton. With the pleasant prancks of Smug
the Smith . . . by T.B., entered in the Stationers' Register in 1608.

MIRTH.

But there was one Smug, a smith, would have made a
horse laugh and broke his halter, as they say.

TATTLE.

Oh, but the poor man had got a shrewd mischance one
day.        70

EXPECTATION.

How, gossip?

TATTLE.

He had dress'd a rogue jade i'the morning that had the
staggers, and had got such a spice of 'em himself by noon
as they would not away all the play time, do what he
could for his heart.        75

MIRTH.

'Twas his part, gossip. He was to be drunk by his part.

TATTLE.

Say you so? I understood not so much.

EXPECTATION.

Would we had such another part and such a man in
this play. I fear 'twill be an excellent dull thing.

CENSURE.

Expect, intend it.        80


[II.i]

[*Enter*] Pennyboy Senior, Pecunia, Mortgage, Statute, Band,
Broker.

PENNYBOY SENIOR.

Your grace is sad, methinks, and melancholy.


72. rogue] *F;* Roguy *F3.*        74. he] *F3;* hec *F.*

---

67. *Smug*] a tippling smith in *The Merry Devil.*
73. *staggers*] a disease of domestic animals in which a staggering
gait is a symptom.
73. *spice*] touch.
74. *play time*] from two o'clock to about four in the afternoon.
80. *intend it*] fix your attention on it.
[II.i]
1. *Your grace*] courtesy title for "Queen Pecunia" (l. 43). Cf. 1. 22.

You do not look upon me with that face
As you were wont, my goddess, bright Pecunia.
Although your grace be fall'n off two i'the hundred
In vulgar estimation, yet am I                         5
Your grace's servant still, and teach this body
To bend and these my aged knees to buckle
In adoration and just worship of you.
Indeed, I do confess, I have no shape
To make a minion of, but I'm your martyr,              10
Your grace's martyr. I can hear the rogues,
As I do walk the streets, whisper and point,
"There goes old Pennyboy, the slave of money,
Rich Pennyboy, Lady Pecunia's drudge,
A sordid rascal, one that never made                   15
Good meal in his sleep but sells the acates are sent him,
Fish, fowl, and venison, and preserves himself,
Like an old hoary rat, with moldy pie crust."
This I do hear, rejoicing I can suffer
This, and much more, for your good grace's sake.       20

PECUNIA.

Why do you so, my guardian? I not bid you.
Cannot my grace be gotten, and held too,
Without your self-tormentings and your watches,
Your macerating of your body thus
With cares and scantings of your diet and rest?        25

PENNYBOY SENIOR.

Oh no, your services, my princely lady,
Cannot with too much zeal of rites be done,
They are so sacred.

4. fall'n off] _Gifford;_ falne, of _F;_     16. Good . . . sells] _F, F3._ Good
faln, of _F3;_ Falne of, _H.S._            meale but in his sleep, sells _Rob-_
6. Your] _F3;_ You _F._                    _ert Nares conj. quoted by H.S._

---

4. _Although . . . hundred_] In 1571 a maximum interest rate of ten
per cent was set; an act of 1624 fixed the rate at eight per cent
(Knights, p. 128).
    10. _minion_] lover.
    15–16. _one . . . sleep_] one who never allows himself the luxury of
even dreaming about eating well.
    16. _acates_] provisions, delicacies.
    22. _grace_] favor.

PECUNIA.                    But my reputation
    May suffer, and the worship of my family,
    When by so servile means they both are sought.              30
PENNYBOY SENIOR.
    You are a noble, young, free, gracious lady
    And would be everybody's in your bounty,
    But you must not be so. They are a few
    That know your merit, lady, and can value't.
    Yourself scarce understands your proper powers.             35
    They are almighty, and that we, your servants,
    That have the honor here to stand so near you,
    Know, and can use too. All this nether world
    Is yours. You command it and do sway it,
    The honor of it and the honesty,                            40
    The reputation, ay, and the religion
    (I was about to say and had not err'd)
    Is Queen Pecunia's. For that style is yours
    If mortals knew your grace, or their own good.
MORTGAGE.
    Please your grace to retire.
BAND.                           I fear your grace                45
    Hath ta'en too much of the sharp air.
PECUNIA.                                    Oh no!
    I could endure to take a great deal more
    (And with my constitution) were it left
    Unto my choice. What think you of it, Statute?
STATUTE.
    A little now and then does well, and keeps                  50
    Your grace in your complexion.
BAND.                           And true temper.

48. constitution)   were   it   left]
*1716;* constitution, were it left) *F,*
*F3.*

---

40–43. *The honor . . . Pecunia's*] parallels the lines in which Plutus
learns of his importance from Chremylus (Aristophanes *Plutus,* ll.
141–46) although the figure of *regina Pecunia* is used by Horace
(*Epistles* 1. 6. 36–37).
    43. *style*] honorific or official title.

MORTGAGE.

    But too much, madam, may increase cold rheums,
    Nourish catarrhs, green sicknesses, and agues,
    And put you in consumption.

PENNYBOY SENIOR.              Best to take

    Advice of your grave women, noble madam.      55
    They know the state o' your body, and ha' studied
    Your grace's health.

BAND.              And honor. Here'll be visitants

    Or suitors by and by, and 'tis not fit
    They find you here.

STATUTE.          'Twill make your grace too cheap

    To give them audience presently.

MORTGAGE.           Leave your secretary    60

    To answer them.

PECUNIA.        Wait you here, Broker.

BROKER.               I shall, madam.

    And do your grace's trusts with diligence.

                    *[Exeunt all but* Broker.]

[II.ii]             *[Enter]* Piedmantle.

PIEDMANTLE.

    What luck's this? I am come an inch too late.
    Do you hear, sir? Is your worship o'the family
    Unto the Lady Pecunia?

BROKER.            I serve her grace, sir,

    Aurelia Clara Pecunia, the Infanta.

PIEDMANTLE.

    Has she all those titles and her grace besides?    5
    I must correct that ignorance and oversight
    Before I do present. Sir, I have drawn
    A pedigree for her grace, though yet a novice
    In that so noble study.

BROKER.         A Herald at Arms?

[II.ii]
0.1.] Piedmantle, Broker, Pennyboy Senior. *F, F3.*

PIEDMANTLE.

    No, sir, a pursuivant. My name is Piedmantle.          10

BROKER.

    Good Master Piedmantle.

PIEDMANTLE.                I have deduc'd her—

BROKER.

    From all the Spanish mines in the West Indies,

    I hope, for she comes that way by her mother;

    But, by her grandmother, she's Duchess of Mines.

PIEDMANTLE.

    From man's creation I have brought her.

BROKER.                    No further?    15

    Before, sir, long before. You have done nothing, else.

    Your mines were before Adam. Search your office,

    Roll five and twenty, you will find it so.

    I see you are but a novice, Master Piedmantle,

    If you had not told me so.

PIEDMANTLE.             Sir, an apprentice    20

    In armory. I have read *The Elements*

    And *Accidence* and all the leading books,

    And I have now upon me a great ambition,

    How to be brought to her grace to kiss her hands.

BROKER.

    Why, if you have acquaintance with Mistress Statute    25

    Or Mistress Band, my lady's gentlewomen,

    They can induce you. One is a judge's daughter

    But somewhat stately; th'other, Mistress Band,

    Her father's but a scrivener, but she can

    Almost as much with my lady as the other,    30

    Especially if Rose Wax the chambermaid

    Be willing. Do you not know her, sir, neither?

15. further] *F;* farther *F3.*

---

10. *pursuivant*] See Persons of the Play, l. 10, note.

11. *deduc'd her*] traced the course of her descent.

21–22. *The Elements . . . Accidence*] *The Elements of Armories*, 1610, by Edmund Bolton, and *The Accidence of Armory*, 1562, by Gerard Leigh; the latter was reprinted as late as 1612.

27. *induce*] introduce.

PIEDMANTLE.

    No, in troth, sir.

BROKER.              She's a good pliant wench
And easy to be wrought, sir. But the nurse,
Old Mother Mortgage, if you have a tenement            35
Or such a morsel? Though she have no teeth,
She loves a sweetmeat, anything that melts
In her warm gums. She could command it for you
On such a trifle, a toy. Sir, you may see
How for your love and this so pure complexion          40
(A perfect sanguine) I ha' ventur'd thus,
The straining of a ward, opening a door
Into the secrets of our family.

PIEDMANTLE.

    I pray you let me know, sir, unto whom
I am so much beholden; but your name.                  45

BROKER.

    My name is Broker. I am secretary
And usher to her grace.

PIEDMANTLE.           Good Master Broker!

BROKER.

    Good Master Piedmantle!

PIEDMANTLE.          Why, you could do me,
If you would now, this favor of yourself.

BROKER.

    Truly, I think I could. But if I would,                 50
I hardly should, without or Mistress Band
Or Mistress Statute please to appear in it,
Or the good nurse I told you of, Mistress Mortgage.
We know our places here. We mingle not
One in another's sphere, but all move orderly           55
In our own orbs, yet we are all concentrics.

---

35. *tenement*] "a portion of a house, tenanted as a separate dwell-
ing" *(OED)*.

41. *sanguine*] A sanguine complexion, the sign of the predominance
of the blood over the other three humors, indicated a courageous,
amorous, and hopeful disposition.

56. *concentrics*] They all revolve around Pecunia.

PIEDMANTLE.

    Well, sir, I'll wait a better season.

BROKER.                        Do,

    And study the right means. Get Mistress Band

    To urge on your behalf, or little Wax.

                      Broker *makes a mouth at him.*

PIEDMANTLE.

    I have a hope, sir, that I may by chance          60

    Light on her grace as she's taking the air.

BROKER.

    That air of hope has blasted many an aiery

    Of kestrels like yourself, good Master Piedmantle.

             *He jeers him again.* [*Exit* Piedmantle.]

           *Old* Pennyboy *leaps* [*out.*]

PENNYBOY SENIOR.

    Well said, Master Secretary. I stood behind

    And heard thee all. I honor thy dispatches.     65

    If they be rude, untrained in our method,

    And have not studied the rule, dismiss 'em quickly.

    Where's Lickfinger my cook, that unctuous rascal?

    He'll never keep his hour, that vessel of kitchen stuff!

[II.iii]               [*Enter*] Lickfinger.

BROKER.

    Here he is come, sir.

[II.ii]              0.1.] Broker, Pennyboy S e n i o r ,
66. in *F3;* it *F.*        Lickfinger. *F, F3.*

---

    61. *Light on*] happen upon; Broker interprets the phrase to mean
"swoop down on."

    62. *aiery*] nest of birds of prey; Gifford's spelling *aiery* where *F*
reads *ayrie* points up the pun.

    63. *kestrels*] small hawks of an inferior kind, windhovers.

    69. *vessel . . . stuff*] container of drippings from roasts, skimming,
etc., sometimes reused in a household and sometimes sold. In
*Bartholomew Fair,* II.v.74, Winwife mocks Ursula's girth by calling
her "an inspir'd vessel of kitchen-stuff."

PENNYBOY SENIOR.          Pox upon him, kidney,
    Always too late!
LICKFINGER.          To wish 'em you, I confess,
    That ha' them already.
PENNYBOY SENIOR.          What?
LICKFINGER                    The pox!
PENNYBOY SENIOR.                    The piles,
    The plague, and all diseases light on him
    Knows not to keep his word. I'd keep my word sure!          5
    I hate that man that will not keep his word.
    When did I break my word?
LICKFINGER.                    Or I, till now?
    And 'tis but half an hour.
PENNYBOY SENIOR.          Half a year,
    To me that stands upon a minute of time.
    I am a just man. I love still to be just.          10
LICKFINGER.
    Why, you think I can run like light-foot Ralph,
    Or keep a wheelbarrow with a sail in town here
    To whirl me to you. I have lost two stone
    Of suet i'the service posting hither.
    You might have followed me like a watering pot          15
    And seen the knots I made along the street.
    My face dropp'd like the skimmer in a fritter pan,
    And my whole body is yet (to say the truth)
    A roasted pound of butter with grated bread in't!

                              *He sweeps his face.*

---

    1. *Pox*] French pox, syphilis.
    11. *light-foot Ralph*] H.S. suggest Lady Bedford's runner, Rafe, "The
Countesses' man who wonne y^e race," the last to be blessed in the
grace that appears as no. xlvii in *Ungathered Verse*, ed. Herford and
Simpson, vol. 8, pp. 418–19.
    13–14. *two stone/ Of suet*] In *Bartholomew Fair*, II.ii.81, Ursula
complains that she dwindles away by this amount daily.
    16. *knots*] figures made by crisscrossing lines.
    19. *roasted . . . bread*] a stiff mixture of butter, sugar, and egg yolks
toasted on a spit and dredged continually with bread crumbs, sugar,
and currants until the butter stops seeping through the crust (Markham, p. 83).

PENNYBOY SENIOR.
    Believe you he that list. You stay'd of purpose,          20
    To have my venison stink and my fowl mortified
    That you might ha' 'em—
LICKFINGER.                        A shilling or two cheaper.
    That's your jealousy.
PENNYBOY SENIOR.          Perhaps it is.
    Will you go in and view and value all?
    Yonder is venison sent me, fowl, and fish,                25
    In such abundance I am sick to see it!
    I wonder what they mean. I ha' told 'em of it.
    To burden a weak stomach and provoke
    A dying appetite, thrust a sin upon me
    I ne'er was guilty of. Nothing but gluttony,              30
    Gross gluttony, that will undo this land!
LICKFINGER.
    And 'bating two i'the hundred.
PENNYBOY SENIOR.                        Ay, that same's
    A crying sin, a fearful damn'd device
    Eats up the poor, devours 'em—
LICKFINGER.                        Sir, take heed
    What you give out.
PENNYBOY SENIOR.          Against your grave great Solons,   35
    Numae Pompilii, they that made that law
    To take away the poor's inheritance?
    It was their portion. I will stand to't.
    And they have robb'd 'em of it, plainly robb'd 'em.
    I still am a just man. I tell the truth.                  40
    When monies went at ten i'the hundred, I
    And such as I, the servants of Pecunia,
    Could spare the poor two out of ten and did it.
    How say you, Broker?
LICKFINGER [aside].          Ask your echo.

---

    20. *list*] chooses.
    23. *jealousy*] suspicion.
    32. *'bating*] i.e., abating. The reference is to the recent decrease in
interest rates. See II.i.4, note.
    36. *Numae Pompilii*] Numa Pompilius was the second of the legen-
dary kings of Rome (715–672 B.C.), whose reign was long and peaceful.

BROKER.                              You did it.
PENNYBOY SENIOR.
    I am for justice. When did I leave justice?      45
    We knew 'twas theirs. They had right and title to't.
    Now—
LICKFINGER.  You can spare 'em nothing.
PENNYBOY SENIOR.                      Very little,
LICKFINGER.
    As good as nothing.
PENNYBOY SENIOR.          They have bound our hands
    With their wise solemn act, shorten'd our arms.
LICKFINGER.
    Beware those worshipful ears, sir, be not shorten'd,    50
    And you play crop i'the Fleet if you use this license.
PENNYBOY SENIOR.
    What license, knave? informer?
LICKFINGER.                          I am Lickfinger,
    Your cook.
PENNYBOY SENIOR.  A saucy Jack you are, that's once.
    What said I, Broker?
BROKER.                  Nothing that I heard, sir.
LICKFINGER.
    I know his gift. He can be deaf when he list.    55
PENNYBOY SENIOR.
    Ha' you provided me my bushel of eggs
    I did bespeak—I do not care how stale
    Or stinking that they be, let 'em be rotten—
    For ammunition here to pelt the boys
    That break my windows?
LICKFINGER.                      Yes, sir, I ha' spar'd 'em    60
    Out of the custard politic for you, the Mayor's.
PENNYBOY SENIOR.
    'Tis well. Go in, take hence all that excess,

---

51. *crop . . . Fleet*] have your ears cropped in Fleet Prison.
53. *Jack*] knave.
53. *that's once*] that settles it.
61. *custard politic*] large enough for the jester to leap into, prepared for the Lord Mayor's feast.

Make what you can of it, you're best. And when
I have friends that I invite at home, provide me
Such, such, and such a dish as I bespeak; 65
One at a time, no superfluity.
Or if you have it not, return me money.
You know my ways.
LICKFINGER.                    They are a little crooked.
PENNYBOY SENIOR.
How, knave?
LICKFINGER.        Because you do indent.
PENNYBOY SENIOR.                        'Tis true, sir,
I do indent you shall return me money. 70
LICKFINGER.
Rather than meat, I know it. You are just still.
PENNYBOY SENIOR.
I love it still. And therefore if you spend
The red-deer pies i'your house or sell 'em forth, sir,
Cast so that I may have their coffins all
Return'd here and pil'd up. I would be thought 75
To keep some kind of house.
LICKFINGER.                        By the moldy signs?
PENNYBOY SENIOR.
And then remember meat for my two dogs:
Fat flaps of mutton, kidneys, rumps of veal,
Good plenteous scraps. My maid shall eat the relics.
LICKFINGER.
When you and your dogs have din'd! A sweet reversion. 80

63. you're] *this edn.;* your *F, F3.*

---

69. *indent*] "a pun on the toothed or wavy line which (1) marked
off the two halves of a legal document drawn up in duplicate, (2)
formed the cut edge of two such separate documents: hence the use
to express drawing up the documents, and finally to enter upon an
agreement" (H.S.).
72. *spend*] consume.
74. *Cast*] contrive, manage.
74. *coffins*] crusts of pies, in which the meat was "buried."
79. *relics*] remnants, leavings.

PENNYBOY SENIOR.

Who's here? My courtier and my little doctor?
My muster-master? And what plover's that
They have brought to pull?

BROKER.                              I know not. Some green plover.

I'll find him out.

PENNYBOY SENIOR.    Do, for I know the rest.
They are the jeerers, mocking, flouting Jacks.          85

[II.iv]    [*Enter*] Fitton, Almanac, Shunfield, Madrigal.

FITTON.

How now, old money-bawd? W'are come—

PENNYBOY SENIOR.                              To jeer me
As you were wont. I know you.

ALMANAC.                              No, to give thee
Some good security and see Pecunia.

PENNYBOY SENIOR.

What is't?

FITTON.          Ourselves.

ALMANAC.                    We'll be one bound for another.

FITTON.

This noble doctor here.

ALMANAC.                    This worthy courtier.          5

FITTON.

This man o' war, he was our muster-master,

ALMANAC.

But a sea captain now, brave Captain Shunfield.
                    *He* [Pennyboy Senior] *holds up his nose.*

[II.iv]
0.1.] Fitton, Pennyboy Senior, Almanac, Shunfield, Madrigal, Lickfinger, Broker. *F, F3.*

---

[II.iii]
82. *muster-master*] officer responsible for the accuracy of the muster-
roll, the register of officers and men in an army or ship's company.
82. *plover*] a slang term for a swindler's victim.

SHUNFIELD.

You snuff the air now, as the scent displeas'd you.

FITTON.

Thou need'st not fear him, man. His credit is sound.

ALMANAC.

And season'd too since he took salt at sea.      10

PENNYBOY SENIOR.

I do not love pickl'd security.
Would I had one good fresh man in for all,
For truth is, you three stink.

SHUNFIELD.          You are a rogue.

PENNYBOY SENIOR.

I think I am, but I will lend no money
On that security, captain.

ALMANAC.          Here's a gentleman,      15
A fresh man i'the world, one Master Madrigal.

         Madrigal *steps aside with* Broker.

FITTON.

Of an untainted credit. What say you to him?

SHUNFIELD.

He's gone, methinks. Where is he? Madrigal?

PENNYBOY SENIOR.

H'has an odd singing name. Is he an heir?

FITTON.

An heir to a fair fortune—

ALMANAC.          And full hopes;      20
A dainty scholar and a pretty poet.

PENNYBOY SENIOR.

Y'ave said enough. I ha' no money, gentlemen,
An' he go to't in rhyme once, not a penny.

         *He snuffs again.*

SHUNFIELD.

Why, he's of years though he have little beard.

PENNYBOY SENIOR.

His beard has time to grow. I have no money.      25
Let him still dabble in poetry. No Pecunia
Is to be seen.

---

8. *snuff*] sniff.

ALMANAC.              Come, thou lov'st to be costive
    Still i' thy court'sy, but I have a pill,
    A' golden pill, to purge away this melancholy.
SHUNFIELD.
    'Tis nothing but his keeping o'the house here                    30
    With his two drowsy dogs.
FITTON.                          A drench of sack
    At a good tavern, and a fine fresh pullet
    Would cure him.
LICKFINGER.          Nothing but a young hare in white broth;
    I know his diet better than the doctor.
SHUNFIELD.
    What, Lickfinger, mine old host of Ram Alley,                    35
    You ha' some market here?
ALMANAC.                          Some dosser of fish
    Or fowl to fetch off?
FITTON.                      An odd bargain of venison
    To drive?
PENNYBOY SENIOR.    Will you go in, knave?
LICKFINGER.                                  I must needs.
    You see who drives me, gentlemen.
                              Pennyboy [Senior] *thrusts him in.*
ALMANAC.                          Not the devil.

33. hare] *this edn.;* Haire *F;* Heir      37. off] *F3;* of *F.*
*F3.*

___

27. *costive*] a pun on "costive" meaning (1) niggardly and (2) con-
stipated.
    29. *golden pill . . . melancholy*] "Pills to purge melancholy, which
D'Urfey afterwards took as a title to his collection of ballads, had
long been a kind of proverbial phrase" (Nares).
    31. *drench*] drink.
    33. *hare*] "Hare" and "heir" were still homophones at the time of
the play.
    35. *Ram Alley*] a court seven feet wide on the south side of Fleet
Street (Sugden); in Barry's *Ram-Alley,* 1611, the lawyer Throat observes that: "Ram-Alley stinks with cooks and ale" (*Dodsley's Old
Plays,* ed. Hazlitt, 10:292).
    36. *dosser*] pannier.
    38-39. *I . . . devil*] proverb: "He must needs go that the devil
drives" (Tilley, D 278).

FITTON.

    He may be in time. He is his agent now.        **40**

PENNYBOY SENIOR.

    You are all cogging Jacks, a covey o' wits,

    The jeerers, that still call together at meals.

    Or rather an aiery, for you are birds of prey

    And fly at all; nothing's too big or high for you.

    And are so truly fear'd, but not belov'd        **45**

    One of another, as no one dares break

    Company from the rest lest they should fall

    Upon him absent.

ALMANAC.               Oh, the only oracle

    That ever peep'd or spake out of a doublet.

SHUNFIELD.

    How the rogue stinks, worse than a fishmonger's sleeves!  **50**

FITTON.

    Or currier's hands!

SHUNFIELD.            And such a parboil'd visage!

FITTON.

    His face looks like a dyer's apron, just!

ALMANAC.

    A sodden head, and his whole brain a posset curd!

PENNYBOY SENIOR.

    Ay, now you jeer, jeer on. I have no money.

ALMANAC.

    I wonder what religion he's of.        **55**

FITTON.

    No certain species sure. A kind of mule,

    That's half an Ethnic, half a Christian.

50. fishmonger's] *F3;* Fishmonger *F.*

---

    41. *cogging Jacks|* cheating knaves.

    41. *covey*] set (originally a family of partridges keeping together during the first season).

    49. *peep'd*] spoke like a ventriloquist (H.S.).

    53. *sodden*] stewed, boiled.

    53. *posset curd*] "hot milk poured on ale or sack, having sugar, grated bisket, and eggs, with other ingredients, boiled in it, which goes all to a curd" (Randle Holme, *Academy of Armourie*, 1688, bk. 3, p. 84).

    57. *Ethnic*] heathen.

PENNYBOY SENIOR.
    I have no money, gentlemen.
SHUNFIELD.                                    This stock,
    He has no sense of any virtue, honor,
    Gentry, or merit.
PENNYBOY SENIOR.          You say very right,                    60
    My meritorious captain (as I take it),
    Merit will keep no house nor pay no house rent.
    Will Mistress Merit go to market, think you,
    Set on the pot or feed the family?
    Will Gentry clear with the butcher or the baker,        65
    Fetch in a pheasant or a brace of partridges
    From goodwife Poulter for my lady's supper?
FITTON.
    See, this pure rogue.
PENNYBOY SENIOR.          This rogue has money though.
    My worshipful brave courtier has no money.
    No, nor my valiant captain.
SHUNFIELD.                              Hang you, rascal!          70
PENNYBOY SENIOR.
    Nor you, my learned doctor. I lov'd you
    While you did hold your practice and kill tripe-wives
    And kept you to your urinal, but since your thumbs
    Have greas'd the ephemerides, casting figures,
    And turning over for your candle-rents,                75
    And your twelve houses in the zodiac,
    With your almutens, almacantaras,
    Troth, you shall cant alone for Pennyboy.

---

58. *stock*] log, block, insensitive person.
72. *tripe-wives*] women who dress and sell tripe.
73. *kept . . . urinal*] analyzed urine as part of medical diagnoses.
74. *ephemerides*] almanacs containing astrological predictions.
75. *turning over*] the almanacs (H.S.).
75. *candle-rents*] "rent or revenue derived from house-property (which is continually undergoing deterioration or waste)" *(OED)*.
77. *almutens*] ruling planets in horoscopes.
77. *almacantaras*] small circles of the sphere parallel to the horizon, cutting the meridian at equal distances.

SHUNFIELD.

    I told you what we should find him, a mere bawd.

FITTON.

    A rogue, a cheater.

PENNYBOY SENIOR.       What you please, gentlemen.      80
    I am of that humble nature and condition
    Never to mind your worships, or take notice
    Of what you throw away thus. I keep house here
    Like a lame cobbler, never out of doors,
    With my two dogs, my friends, and (as you say)      85
    Drive a quick pretty trade still. I get money.
    And as for titles, be they rogue or rascal
    Or what your worships fancy, let 'em pass
    As transitory things. They're mine today
    And yours tomorrow.

ALMANAC.              Hang thee, dog!

SHUNFIELD.                   Thou cur!      90

PENNYBOY SENIOR.

    You see how I do blush and am asham'd
    Of these large attributes? Yet you have no money.

ALMANAC.

    Well wolf, hyena, you old pocky rascal,
    You will ha' the hernia fall down again
    Into your scrotum, and I shall be sent for.      95
    I will remember then, that, and your fistula
    *In ano* I cur'd you of.

PENNYBOY SENIOR.       Thank your dog-leech craft!
    They were wholesome piles afore you meddl'd with 'em.

ALMANAC.

    What an ungrateful wretch is this!

---

    79. *mere*] absolute.

    92. *large*] gross.

    97. *dog-leech craft*] "In the days of bear-baiting and bull-baiting, the poor dogs had a sorry time of it, and their 'leaches' on the bank [the Bankside, where the bear-baiting arenas were located] drove a roaring trade. In the opening scene of the Alchemist . . . 'dog-leach' is one of the worst terms of abuse Face can find for Subtle" (Cunningham).

SHUNFIELD.                            He minds
   A courtesy no more than London Bridge                    100
   What arch was mended last.
FITTON.                               He never thinks
   More than a log of any grace at court
   A man may do him, or that such a lord
   Reach'd him his hand.
PENNYBOY SENIOR.                    Oh yes! If grace would strike
   The brewer's tally, or my good lord's hand                    105
   Would quit the scores. But sir, they will not do it.
   Here's a piece. My good Lord Piece doth all.
                      *He shows a piece [of gold].*
   Goes to the butcher's, fetches in a mutton,
   Then to the baker's, brings in bread, makes fires,
   Gets wine, and does more real courtesies                    110
   Than all my lords, I know. My sweet Lord Piece,
   You are my lord; the rest are cogging Jacks,
   Under the rose.
SHUNFIELD.             Rogue, I could beat you now.
PENNYBOY SENIOR.
   True, captain, if you durst beat any other,
   I should believe you. But indeed you are hungry,                    115
   You are not angry, captain, if I know you
   Aright, good captain. No Pecunia
   Is to be seen though Mistress Band would speak,
   Or little Blushet-Wax be ne'er so easy.
   I'll stop mine ears with her against the sirens,                    120
   Court and philosophy. God be wi' you, gentlemen.
   Provide you better names, Pecunia is for you.        *[Exit.]*
FITTON.
   What a damn'd harpy it is. Where's Madrigal?
   Is he sneak'd hence?

108. butcher's] *F3;* Butehers *F.*

---

104. *strike*] cancel.
113. *Under the rose*] in secret (L. *sub rosa);* i.e., I tell you in confidence (Tilley, R 185).
119. *Blushet-*] blusher.

SHUNFIELD.                    Here he comes with Broker,
　　Pecunia's secretary.
　　　　　　Madrigal *returns* [*with* Broker].
ALMANAC.                    He may do some good          125
　　With him perhaps. —Where ha' you been, Madrigal?
MADRIGAL.
　　Above with my lady's women, reading verses.
FITTON.
　　That was a favor. Good morrow, Master Secretary.
SHUNFIELD.
　　Good morrow, Master Usher.
ALMANAC.                              Sir, by both
　　Your worshipful titles, and your name Mas Broker,          130
　　Good morrow.
MADRIGAL.          I did ask him if he were
　　Amphibion Broker.
SHUNFIELD.          Why?
MADRIGAL.                              A creature of two natures
　　Because he has two offices.
BROKER.                              You may jeer,
　　You ha' the wits, young gentlemen. But your hope
　　Of Helicon will never carry it here          135
　　With our fat family. We ha' the dullest,
　　Most unbor'd ears for verse amongst our females.
　　I griev'd you read so long, sir. Old Nurse Mortgage,
　　She snor'd i'the chair, and Statute (if you mark'd her)
　　Fell fast alseep, and Mistress Band, she nodded,          140
　　But not with any consent to what you read.
　　They must have somewhat else to chink than rhymes.
　　If you could make an epitaph on your land
　　(Imagine it on departure), such a poem
　　Would wake 'em and bring Wax to her true temper.          145

132. S.P. MADRIGAL] *Whalley;* Alm.
F, F3.

---

130. *Mas*] vulgar shortening of Master.
136. *fat*] complacent.
144. *on departure*] on the point of departing from you.

MADRIGAL.
    I'faith, sir, and I will try.
BROKER.                              'Tis but earth,
    Fit to make bricks and tiles of.
SHUNFIELD.                         Pox upon't.
    'Tis but for pots or pipkins at the best.
    If it would keep us in good tobacco pipes—
BROKER.
    'Twere worth keeping.
FITTON.                         Or in porc'lain dishes,                    150
    There were some hope.
ALMANAC.                         But this is a hungry soil
    And must be help'd.
FITTON.                         Who would hold any land
    To have the trouble to marl it?
SHUNFIELD.                              Not a gentleman.
BROKER.
    Let clowns and hinds affect it, that love ploughs
    And carts and harrows, and are busy still                    155
    In vexing the dull element.
ALMANAC.                         Our sweet songster
    Shall rarify't into air.
FITTON.                         And you, Mas Broker,
    Shall have a feeling.
BROKER.                         So it supple, sir,
    The nerves.
MADRIGAL.         Oh, it shall be palpable,
    Make thee run through a hoop or a thumb-ring,                    160
    The nose of a tobacco pipe, and draw
    Thy ductile bones out like a knitting needle
    To serve my subtle turns.
BROKER.                         I shall obey, sir,
    And run a thread like an hourglass.

       [Re-enter Pennyboy Senior.]

---

154. *clowns and hinds*] countrymen and rustics.
154. *affect*] seek.
158. *a feeling*] a tip, a bribe.

PENNYBOY SENIOR.                              Where is Broker?

Are not these flies gone yet? Pray quit my house.          165
I'll smoke you out else.

FITTON.                              Oh, the prodigal!

Will you be at so much charge with us and loss?

MADRIGAL.

I have heard you ha' offered, sir, to lock up smoke
And caulk your windores, spar up all your doors,
Thinking to keep it a close prisoner wi' you,          170
And wept when it went out, sir, at your chimney.

FITTON.

And yet his eyes were drier than a pumice.

SHUNFIELD.

A wretched rascal, that will bind about
The nose of his bellows, lest the wind get out
When he's abroad.

ALMANAC.                          Sweeps down no cobwebs here          175
But sells 'em for cut fingers, and the spiders,
As creatures rear'd of dust and cost him nothing,
To fat old ladies' monkeys.

FITTON.                              He has offer'd
To gather up spill'd water, and preserve
Each hair falls from him to stop balls withal.          180

SHUNFIELD.

A slave and an idolator to Pecunia!

PENNYBOY SENIOR.

You all have happy memories, gentlemen,
In rocking my poor cradle. I remember, too,

---

168. offered] F; offer'd F3.          180. withal] F3; with all F.
169. windores] F; Windows F3.

---

168–80. I . . . withal] a free adaptation of Pythadodicus' examples
of the miserliness of Euclio in Plautus' Pot of Gold, ll. 299–313.
    169. windores] windows.
    169. spar up] bolt or bar.
    180. stop] stuff.
    180. balls] tennis balls.

When you had lands and credit, worship, friends,
Ay, and could give security. Now, you have none,        185
Or will have none right shortly. This can time
And the vicissitude of things. I have
All these and money, too, and do possess 'em,
And am right heartily glad of all our memories
And both the changes.
FITTON.                    Let us leave the viper.        190
        [*Exeunt all but* Pennyboy Senior *and* Broker.]
PENNYBOY SENIOR.
He's glad he is rid of his torture, and so soon.
Broker, come hither. Up, and tell your lady
She must be ready presently, and Statute,
Band, Mortgage, Wax. My prodigal young kinsman
Will straight be here to see her, top of our house,        195
The flourishing and flaunting Pennyboy.
We were but three of us in all the world.
My brother Francis, whom they call'd Frank Pennyboy,
Father to this; he's dead. This Pennyboy
Is now the heir. I, Richer Pennyboy,        200
Not Richard, but old Harry Pennyboy,
And (to make rhyme) close, wary Pennyboy.
I shall have all at last, my hopes do tell me.
Go, see all ready. And where my dogs have faulted,
Remove it with a broom and sweeten all        205
With a slice of juniper, not too much, but sparing.
We may be faulty ourselves else and turn prodigal
In entertaining of the prodigal.        [*Exit* Broker.]
Here he is and with him—what? A clapper dudgeon!
That's a good sign, to have the beggar follow him        210
So near at his first entry into fortune.

---

206. *slice*] fire shovel *(OED)*.
206. *juniper*] burned to purify the air.
209. *clapper dudgeon*] beggar-born; Skeat conjectures the derivation
as *clapper,* the lid of a beggar's clap dish, and *dudgeon,* a kind of
wood of which knife handles were made (*Glossary of Tudor and Stuart
Words* [Oxford, 1914]).

[II.v] [*Enter*] Pennyboy Junior, Pennyboy Canter, Picklock.

PENNYBOY JUNIOR.
> How now, old uncle? I am come to see thee
> And the brave lady here, the daughter of Ophir,
> They say thou keep'st.

PENNYBOY SENIOR.                    Sweet nephew, if she were
> The daughter o'the Sun, she's at your service
> And so am I and the whole family,                          5
> Worshipful nephew.

PENNYBOY JUNIOR.          Say'st thou so, dear uncle?
> Welcome my friends then. Here is Domine Picklock,
> My man o' law, solicits all my causes,
> Follows my business, makes and compounds my quarrels
> Between my tenants and me, sows all my strifes          10
> And reaps them too, troubles the country for me
> And vexes any neighbor that I please.

PENNYBOY SENIOR.
> But with commission?

PENNYBOY JUNIOR.                Under my hand and seal.

PENNYBOY SENIOR.
> A worshipful place!

PICKLOCK.                    I thank his worship for it.

PENNYBOY SENIOR.
> But what is this old gentleman?

PENNYBOY CANTER.                        A rogue,          15
> A very canter I, sir, one that maunds
> Upon the pad. We should be brothers though,
> For you are near as wretched as myself.
> You dare not use your money, and I have none.

0.1.] Pennyboy Junior, Pennyboy
Senior, Picklock, Canter) Broker,
Pecunia, Statute, Band, Wax,
Mortgage *hid in the study. F, F3.*

---

2. *Ophir*] See I.vi.43, note.
15. *rogue*] confirmed vagrant.
16. *maunds*] begs (slang).
17. *pad*] way or road (slang).

PENNYBOY SENIOR.
    Not use my money, cogging Jack? Who uses it     20
    At better rates, lets it for more i'the hundred
    Than I do, sirrah?
PENNYBOY JUNIOR.     Be not angry, uncle.
PENNYBOY SENIOR.
    What, to disgrace me with my queen as if
    I did not know her value?
PENNYBOY CANTER.     Sir, I meant
    You durst not to enjoy it.
PENNYBOY SENIOR.     Hold your peace,     25
    You are a Jack.
PENNYBOY JUNIOR.  Uncle, he shall be a John
    An' you go to that, as good a man as you are.
                       *Young* Pennyboy *is angry.*
    An' I can make him so, a better man.
    Perhaps I will too. Come, let us go.
PENNYBOY SENIOR.     Nay, kinsman,
    My worshipful kinsman and the top of our house,     30
    Do not your penitent uncle that affront,
    For a rash word to leave his joyful threshold
    Before you see the lady that you long for,
    The Venus of the time and state, Pecunia!
    I do perceive your bounty loves the man     35
    For some concealed virtue that he hides
    Under those rags.
PENNYBOY CANTER.   I owe my happiness to him,
    The waiting on his worship since I brought him
    The happy news welcome to all young heirs.
PENNYBOY JUNIOR.
    Thou didst indeed, for which I thank thee yet.     40
    Your fortunate princess, uncle, is long a-coming.
PENNYBOY CANTER.
    She is not rigg'd, sir. Setting forth some lady

26. S.P.] *F3;* P. Se. *F.*        27. An'] *1716;* And *F, F3.*

---

   26. *a John*] i.e., a servant to me.

> Will cost as much as furnishing a fleet.
> Here she's come at last, and like a galley
> Gilt i'the prow.

*The Study is open'd where she* [Pecunia] *sits in state* [*attended by* Broker, Statute, Band, Wax, *and* Mortgage].

PENNYBOY JUNIOR.  Is this Pecunia?                          45
PENNYBOY SENIOR.
    Vouchsafe my toward kinsman, gracious madam,
    The favor of your hand.
PECUNIA.                              Nay, of my lips, sir,
    To him.                                    *She kisseth him.*
PENNYBOY JUNIOR.  She kisses like a mortal creature.
    Almighty madam, I have long'd to see you.
PECUNIA.
    And I have my desire, sir, to behold                50
    That youth and shape which in my dreams and wakes
    I have so oft contemplated and felt
    Warm in my veins and native as my blood.
    When I was told of your arrival here,
    I felt my heart beat as it would leap out            55
    In speech, and all my face it was a flame,
    But how it came to pass I do not know.
PENNYBOY JUNIOR.
    Oh, beauty loves to be more proud than nature,
    That made you blush. I cannot satisfy
    My curious eyes, by which alone I am happy,          60
    In my beholding you.                    *He kisseth her.*
PENNYBOY CANTER.            They pass the compliment
    Prettily well.
PICKLOCK.            Ay, he does kiss her. I like him.
PENNYBOY JUNIOR.
    My passion was clear contrary and doubtful.

45. S.D. sits] *F3;* sit *F.*          60. I am] *F;* I'm *F3.*

---

43. *cost . . . fleet*] a topical allusion to the huge amounts of money that Buckingham, as Lord High Admiral, had required to outfit a fleet to sail against Cadiz in 1625.
45. S.D. *The Study*] an enclosed area on the stage (technical term).

I shook for fear, and yet I danc'd for joy.
I had such motions as the sunbeams make          65
Against a wall or playing on a water,
Or trembling vapor of a boiling pot—

PENNYBOY SENIOR.

That's not so good. It should ha' been a crucible
With molten metal, she had understood it.

PENNYBOY JUNIOR.

I cannot talk, but I can love you, madam.          70
Are these your gentlewomen? I love them too.
                    [*He kisseth the* Gentlewomen.]
And which is Mistress Statute? Mistress Band?
They all kiss close. The last stuck to my lips.

BROKER.

It was my lady's chambermaid, soft Wax.

PENNYBOY JUNIOR.

Soft lips she has, I am sure on't. Mother Mortgage     75
I'll owe a kiss till she be younger. Statute,
Sweet Mistress Band, and honey, little Wax,
We must be better acquainted.
            *He doubles the compliment to them all.*

STATUTE.                    We are but servants, sir.

BAND.

But whom her grace is so content to grace,
We shall observe—

WAX.                    And with all fit respect—          80

MORTGAGE.

In our poor places—

WAX.                    Being her grace's shadows.

PENNYBOY JUNIOR.

A fine well-spoken family. What's thy name?

BROKER.

Broker.

---

73–74. *close* . . . *Wax*] "As close as wax" is a proverbial simile
(Tilley, W 134).
    78. S.D. *He* . . . *all*] i.e., he kisses them again.

PENNYBOY JUNIOR [*aside to* Broker].   Methinks my uncle should
    not need thee,
    Who is a crafty knave enough, believe it.
    Art thou her grace's steward?
BROKER.                        No, her usher, sir.            85
PENNYBOY JUNIOR.
    What, o'the hall? Thou hast a sweeping face.
    Thy beard is like a broom.
BROKER.                        No barren chin, sir.
    I am no eunuch though a gentleman-usher.
PENNYBOY JUNIOR.
    Thou shalt go with us. Uncle, I must have
    My princess forth today.
PENNYBOY SENIOR.         Whither you please, sir,            90
    You shall command her.
PECUNIA.                I will do all grace
    To my new servant.
PENNYBOY SENIOR.        Thanks unto your bounty.
    He is my nephew and my chief, the point,
    Tip, top, and tuft of all our family!
    But, sir, condition'd always you return               95
    Statute and Band home, with my sweet, soft Wax,
    And my good nurse here, Mortgage.
PENNYBOY JUNIOR.                        Oh, what else?
PENNYBOY SENIOR.
    By Broker.
PENNYBOY JUNIOR.   Do not fear.
PENNYBOY SENIOR.                She shall go wi' you
    Whither you please, sir, anywhere.
PENNYBOY CANTER.                        I see
    A money-bawd is lightly a flesh-bawd too.            100

93–97.] *F prints in margin:* "Old
Peny-boy *thankes her, but makes
his condition.*"

---

    83–84. *Methinks . . . enough*] proverb: "A crafty knave needs no
broker" (Tilley, K 122).
    94. *tuft*] a nonce word meaning chief or head.
    100. *lightly*] commonly, often.

PICKLOCK.

    Are you advis'd? Now o' my faith, this **Canter**
    Would make a good grave burgess in some barn.

PENNYBOY JUNIOR.

    Come, thou shalt go with us, uncle.

PENNYBOY SENIOR.                    By no means, sir.

PENNYBOY JUNIOR.

    We'll have both sack and fiddlers.

PENNYBOY SENIOR.                    I'll not draw
    That charge upon your worship.

PENNYBOY CANTER.                    He speaks modestly,    105
    And like an uncle.

PENNYBOY SENIOR.       But Mas Broker, here,
    He shall attend you, nephew, her grace's usher.
    And what you fancy to bestow on him,
    Be not too lavish, use a temperate bounty,
    I'll take it to myself.

PENNYBOY JUNIOR.       I will be princely          110
    While I possess my princess, my Pecunia.

PENNYBOY SENIOR.

    Where is't you eat?

PENNYBOY JUNIOR.       Hard by, at Picklock's lodging.
    Old Lickfinger's the cook, here in Ram Alley.

PENNYBOY SENIOR.

    He has good cheer. Perhaps I'll come and see you.

PENNYBOY CANTER.

    Oh, fie! An alley and a cook's shop, gross,          115
    'Twill savor, sir, most rankly of 'em both.
    Let your meat rather follow you to a tavern.
         *The* Canter *takes him aside, and persuades him.*

103. S.P. PENNYBOY SENIOR] *Whal-*
*ley;* P. Ca. *F, F3.*

---

    101. *Are you advis'd?*] has it struck you?
    112–13. *Picklock's . . . Alley*] Throat, the lawyer in Barry's *Ram-
Alley,* 1611, also lives near the Alley (*Dodsley's Old Plays,* ed. Hazlitt,
10: 292).
    114. *cheer*] fare.
    115–16. *alley . . . both*] See II.iv.35, note.

PICKLOCK.

A tavern's as unfit, too, for a princess.

PENNYBOY CANTER.

No, I have known a princess, and a great one,
Come forth of a tavern.

PICKLOCK.                    Not go in, sir, though.          120

PENNYBOY CANTER.

She must go in if she came forth. The blessed
Pocahontas (as the historian calls her)
And great king's daughter of Virginia
Hath been in womb of a tavern. And besides,
Your nasty uncle will spoil all your mirth          125
And be as noisome.

PICKLOCK.                    That's true.

PENNYBOY CANTER.                              No, faith,
Dine in Apollo with Pecunia,
At brave Duke Wadloe's, have your friends about you
And make a day on't.

PENNYBOY JUNIOR.               Content i'faith.
Our meat shall be brought thither. Simon the king          130
Will bid us welcome.

PICKLOCK.                    Patron, I have a suit.

PENNYBOY JUNIOR.

What's that?

122. her)] *this edn.;* her *F, F3*.          123. daughter of Virginia] *Gifford;*
                                               Daughter of *Virginia) F3;* daugh-
                                               ters of *Virginia F.*

---

122. *historian*] Captain John Smith, author of *The Generall Historie
of Virginia,* 1624.

124. *in womb of*] inside of (?).

124. *tavern*] at Deptford, during Pocahontas' visit to England during
the reign of King James (H. S.).

126. *noisome*] disagreeable.

127. *Apollo*] the room of that name at Dunstan's or the Devil
Tavern, the meeting place of the sons of Ben.

128. *Duke Wadloe's*] Simon Wadloe was innkeeper at Dunstan's.

130. *Simon the king*] the tippling host, "with his ale-dropt hose, &
his malmesy nose," in the song "Old Simon the King," which is printed
in *Bishop Percy's Folio Manuscript: Loose and Humorous Songs,* ed.
J. W. Hales and F. J. Furnivall, 1868, p. 124.

PICKLOCK.          That you will carry the Infanta
    To see the Staple. Her grace will be a grace
    To all the members of it.
PENNYBOY JUNIOR.               I will do it,
    And have her arms set up there with her titles,          135
    Aurelia Clara Pecunia, the Infanta.
    And in Apollo. Come, sweet princess, go.
PENNYBOY SENIOR.
    Broker, be careful of your charge.
BROKER.                         I warrant you.    [*Exeunt.*]

## THE SECOND INTERMEAN AFTER THE SECOND ACT

CENSURE.
    Why, this is duller and duller, intolerable, scurvy!
    Neither devil nor fool in this play! Pray God, some on
    us be not a witch, gossip, to forespeak the matter thus.
MIRTH.
    I fear we are all such, and we were old enough, but we
    are not all old enough to make one witch. How like       5
    you the Vice i'the play?
EXPECTATION.
    Which is he?
MIRTH.
    Three or four: Old covetousness, the sordid Pennyboy,
    the money-bawd who is a flesh-bawd, too, they say.
TATTLE.
    But here is never a fiend to carry him away. Besides he   10
    has never a wooden dagger! I'd not give a rush for a
    Vice that has not a wooden dagger to snap at everybody
    he meets.
MIRTH.
    That was the old way, gossip, when Iniquity came in

───────────────────────────────

[II.v]
    135. *arms . . . titles*] "It was the custom for foreign princes and
noblemen of high rank or office, to set up their arms and titles in
the places through which they passed, or the inns in which they
lodged" (Gifford).

like Hokos Pokos in a juggler's jerkin, with false skirts,    15
like the knave of clubs! But now they are attir'd like
men and women o'the time, the Vices, male and female!
Prodigality, like a young heir, and his mistress Money
(whose favors he scatters like counters), prank'd up like
a prime lady, the Infanta of the Mines.                        20

CENSURE.

Ay, therein they abuse an honorable princess, it is
thought.

MIRTH.

By whom is it so thought? Or where lies the abuse?

CENSURE.

Plain in the styling her Infanta and giving her three
names.                                                         25

MIRTH.

Take heed it lie not in the vice of your interpretation.
What have Aurelia, Clara, Pecunia to do with any
person? Do they any more but express the property of
money, which is the daughter of earth and drawn out
of the mines? Is there nothing to be call'd Infanta but    30
what is subject to exception? Why not the Infanta of
the Beggars or Infanta o'the Gypsies as well as King of
Beggars and King of Gypsies?

CENSURE.

Well, and there were no wiser than I, I would sew him
in a sack and send him by sea to his princess.               35

MIRTH.

Faith, and he heard you, Censure, he would go near to
stick the ass's ears to your high dressing, and perhaps
to all ours for hearkening to you.

TATTLE.

By'r Lady, but he should not to mine. I would hearken
and hearken and censure if I saw cause for th'other     40
princess' sake. Pocahontas, surnam'd the blessed, whom
he has abus'd indeed (and I do censure him and will

---

15. *Hokos Pokos*] appellation of a juggler.

24–25. *three names*] The Infanta of Spain who was the daughter of
Philip II was named Isabella Clara Eugenia.

37. *high dressing*] hair style in which the hair was combed very high.

censure him); to say she came forth of a tavern was
said like a paltry poet.

MIRTH.

That's but one gossip's opinion, and my gossip Tattle's   45
too! But what says Expectation here? She sits sullen
and silent.

EXPECTATION.

Troth, I expect their Office, their great Office, the
Staple, what it will be! They have talk'd on't, but we
see't not open yet. Would Butter would come in and   50
spread itself a little to us.

MIRTH.

Or the butter-box, Buz, the emissary.

TATTLE.

When it is churn'd and dish'd, we shall hear of it.

EXPECTATION.

If it be fresh and sweet butter; but say it be sour and
wheyish?                                                     55

MIRTH.

Then it is worth nothing, mere pot butter, fit to be
spent in suppositories or greasing coach wheels, stale
stinking butter, and such I fear it is, by the being
barrel'd up so long.

EXPECTATION.

Or rank Irish butter.                                     60

CENSURE.

Have patience, gossips. Say that contrary to our expec-
tations it prove right, seasonable, salt butter—

MIRTH.

—Or to the time of year, in Lent, delicate almond butter!
I have a sweet tooth yet, and I will hope the best and
sit down as quiet and calm as butter, look as smooth and   65
soft as butter, be merry and melt like butter, laugh and

---

52. *butter-box*] nickname for a Dutchman.

63. *almond butter*] confection made of almonds, sugar, and rose-
water, recipes for which abound in early English cookbooks. Although
Henry VIII's proclamation in 1538 permitted the use of white meats
in Lent, such substitutes for dairy products remained popular.

be fat like butter, so butter answer my expectation and
be not mad butter. If it be, it shall both July and
December see. I say no more, but—*Dixi.*

---

68–69. *mad . . . December*] proverb: "Butter is mad twice a year"
(Tilley, B 772); "once in summer time in very hot weather, when it
is too thin and fluid, and once in winter in very cold weather, when
it is too hard and difficult to spread" (Ray).

69. *Dixi*] I have spoken; a legal term used by a Roman Praetor to
conclude his speech and indicate that he had pronounced a judgment.

# TO THE READERS

In this following Act, the Office is open'd and show'n to the Prodigal and his Princess Pecunia, wherein the allegory and purpose of the author hath hitherto been wholly mistaken, and so sinister an interpretation been made as if the souls of most of the spectators had liv'd in the eyes and ears of   5
these ridiculous gossips that tattle between the Acts. But he prays you thus to mend it. To consider the news here vented to be none of his news or any reasonable man's, but news made like the time's news (a weekly cheat to draw money) and could not be fitter reprehended than in raising this ri-   1C
diculous Office of the Staple, wherein the age may see her own folly or hunger and thirst after publish'd pamphlets of news, set out every Saturday but made all at home, and no syllable of truth in them, than which there cannot be a greater disease in nature, or a fouler scorn put upon the times. And so ap-   15
prehending it, you shall do the author, and your own judgment, a courtesy, and perceive the trick of alluring money to the Office and there coz'ning the people. If you have the truth, rest quiet, and consider that

    *Ficta voluptatis causa, sint proxima veris.*   20

---

20. *Ficta . . . veris*] Jonson translates as "*Poet* never credit gain'd/ By writing truths, but things (like truths) well fain'd," *Epicoene,* Another Prologue: Occasion'd by some persons impertinent exception, ll. 9–10. Jonson also used this Horatian precept as the epigraph for *The Devil is an Ass.*

[III.i]            *[Enter]* Fitton *[and]* Cymbal.

FITTON.

    You hunt upon a wrong scent still, and think
    The air of things will carry 'em, but it must
    Be reason and proportion, not fine sounds,
    My cousin Cymbal, must get you this lady.
    You have entertain'd a pettifogger here,            5
    Picklock, with trust of an emissary's place,
    And he is all for the young prodigal.
    You see he has left us.
CYMBAL.                          Come, you do not know him
    That speak thus of him.  He will have a trick
    To open us a gap by a trap-door            10
    When they least dream on't.  Here he comes.

                    *[Enter* Picklock.]

                                    What news?

PICKLOCK.

    Where is my brother Buz, my brother Ambler,
    The Register, Examiner, and the clerks?
    Appear, and let us muster all in pomp,
    For here will be the rich Infanta presently            15
    To make her visit.  Pennyboy the heir,
    My patron, has got leave for her to play
    With all her train, of the old churl her guardian.
    Now is your time to make all court unto her,
    That she may first but know then love the place            20
    And show it by her frequent visits here;
    And afterwards get her to sojourn with you.
    She will be weary of the prodigal quickly.
CYMBAL.

    Excellent news!
FITTON.                    And counsel of an oracle!

0.1.] Fitton, Cymbal, *to them* Picklock, Register, Clerk, Thomas
Barber. *F, F3.*

---

    5. *pettifogger*] lawyer of inferior status, one who conducts petty
cases.

CYMBAL.

    How say you, cousin Fitton?

FITTON.                      Brother Picklock,      25

    I shall adore thee for this parcel of tidings.

    It will cry up the credit of our Office

    Eternally, and make our Staple inmortal!

PICKLOCK.

    Look your addresses then be fair and fit,

    And entertain her and her creatures, too,      30

    With all the migniardise and quaint caresses

    You can put on 'em.

FITTON.                 Thou seem'st by thy language

    No less a courtier than a man o' law.

    I must embrace thee.

PICKLOCK.           Tut, I am Vertumnus,

    On every change or chance, upon occasion,     35

    A true chameleon. I can color for't.

    I move upon my axle like a turnpike,

    Fit my face to the parties, and become

    Straight one of them.

      [*Enter* Nathaniel, Thomas Barber, *and* Register.]

CYMBAL.           Sirs, up into your desks

    And spread the rolls upon the table, so.      40

    Is the Examiner set?

REGISTER.        Yes, sir.

CYMBAL.             Ambler and Buz

    Are both abroad now.

PICKLOCK.         We'll sustain their parts.

    No matter, let them ply the affairs without.

39. S.D.] *Gifford.*

---

    31. *migniardise*] "quaintnesse, neatnesse, daintinesse, delicacie, wantonnesse; smooth or fair speech, kind usage" (Cotgrave, *A Dictionairie of the French and English Tongues,* 1611).

    34. *Vertumnus*] Roman god of change, who disguised himself as reaper, gardener, soldier, fisherman, and finally old woman before he was successful in wooing Pomona.

    37. *turnpike*] turnstile.

Let us alone within, I like that well.
On with the cloak, and you with the Staple gown,          45

*Fitton puts on the Office cloak and Cymbal the gown.*

And keep your state, stoop only to the Infanta.
We'll have a flight at Mortgage, Statute, Band,
And hard but we'll bring Wax unto the retrieve.
Each know his several province and discharge it.

FITTON.
I do admire this nimble engine, Picklock.

CYMBAL.                                        Cuz,          50
What did I say?

FITTON.                        You have rectified my error!

*Fitton is brought about.*


[III.ii]

[*Enter*] Pennyboy Junior, Pennyboy Canter, Pecunia, Statute,
Band, Mortgage, Wax, Broker.

PENNYBOY JUNIOR.
By your leave, gentlemen, what news?  Good, good still,
I' your new Office?  Princess, here's the Staple.
This is the governor.  Kiss him, noble princess,
For my sake.                        [*Pecunia kisses Cymbal.*]
          Tom, how is it, honest Tom?
How does thy place, and thou?  My creature, princess,      5
This is my creature.  Give him your hand to kiss.
                              [*Tom kisses Pecunia's hand.*]
He was my barber, now he writes *Clericus!*
I bought this place for him and gave it him.

0.1.] Pennyboy Junior, Pennyboy       5–7.] F *prints in margin: Hee tells*
Canter, Pecunia, Statute, Band,       Pecunia *of* Thom.
Mortgage, Wax, Broker, Custom-
ers. *F, F3.*

---

[III.i]
    48. *And hard*] and it shall go hard.
    48. *retrieve*] recovery of game which has been sprung.
    50. *engine*] plot, trickery.
[III.ii]
    7. *writes*] signs himself.

PENNYBOY CANTER.

    He should have spoke of that, sir, and not you.

    Two do not do one office well.

PENNYBOY JUNIOR.               'Tis true,         10

    But I am loath to lose my courtesies.

PENNYBOY CANTER.

    So are all they that do them to vain ends.

    And yet you do lose when you pay yourselves.

PENNYBOY JUNIOR.

    No more o' your sentences, Canter, they are stale.

    We come for news, remember where you are.      15

    I pray thee let my princess hear some news,

    Good Master Cymbal.

CYMBAL.             What news would she hear?

    Or of what kind, sir?

PENNYBOY JUNIOR.       Any, any kind,

    So it be news, the newest that thou hast,

    Some news of state, for a princess.

CYMBAL.            Read from Rome there.  20

THOMAS BARBER.

    They write, the King of Spain is chosen Pope.

PENNYBOY JUNIOR.             How?

THOMAS BARBER.

    And Emperor, too, the thirtieth of February.

PENNYBOY JUNIOR.

    Is the Emperor dead?

CYMBAL.         No, but he has resign'd

    And trails a pike now under Tilly.

FITTON.             For penance.

PENNYBOY JUNIOR.

    These will beget strange turns in Christendom!  25

13. yourselves] *F3;* you selues *F.*    23–25.] *F margin: "Newes of the*
20–21.] *F margin: "Newes from*   Emperor, *and* Tilly."
Rome."

---

  14. *sentences*] *sententiae,* maxims.

  21. *King of Spain*] Philip IV (1621–65).

  23. *Emperor*] Ferdinand II, Holy Roman Emperor.

  24. *trails a pike*] serves as a soldier.

  24. *Tilly*] Johann Tzerclaes, Count of Tilly, general of the army of
the Catholic League during the first half of the Thirty Years War.

THOMAS BARBER.

And Spinola is made General of the Jesuits.

PENNYBOY JUNIOR.

Stranger!

FITTON.            Sir, all are alike true and certain.

CYMBAL.

All the pretense to the Fifth Monarchy
Was held but vain until the ecclesiastic
And secular powers were united thus                     30
Both in one person.

FITTON.                        'T has been long the aim
Of the house of Austria.

CYMBAL.                        See but Maximilian
His letters to the Baron of Bouttersheim
Or Scheiter-huyssen.

FITTON.                        No, of Liechtenstein,
Lord Paul, I think.

PENNYBOY JUNIOR.        I have heard of some such thing.      35
Don Spinola made General of the Jesuits,
A priest!

CYMBAL.        Oh no, he is dispens'd withal,

---

26–27.] *F margin: "Newes of* Spinola."
28–33.] *F margin: "The fifth* Monarchy, *vniting the* Ecclesiasticke
*and* Secular *power."*

34–36]. *F margin: "A plot of the
house of* Austria."
37. withal] *F3;* with all *F. F prints
in margin: "More of* Spinola."

---

26. *Spinola*] See I.iv.6, note. H.S. query this as "a reproduction of
some inane gossip due to a confusion with Father Spinola the Jesuit
(1564–1622) martyred at Nagasaki on September 20, 1622."

28. *Fifth Monarchy*] the monarchy which, according to a literal
interpretation of Daniel's prophecy, was to succeed the four great
monarchies of Antichrist: Assyria, Persia, Greece, and Rome. Christ
was to be its king and reign a thousand years on earth (Daniel 7–8).

32. *Maximilian*] Duke of Bavier (Bavaria), founder of the Catholic
League. In the Thirty Years War he supported the cause of Ferdinand
II against King James's son-in-law, the Elector-Palatine Frederick V.

33–34. *Bouttersheim . . . Scheiter-huyssen*] fictional Dutch towns,
the first pointing up the Dutch love of butter, the second, a cognate
with the English, meaning privies.

And the whole Society, who do now appear
The only engineers of Christendom.

PENNYBOY JUNIOR.

They have been thought so long, and rightly too.     40

FITTON.

Witness the engine that they have presented him
To wind himself with up into the moon
And thence make all his discoveries.

CYMBAL.                         Read on.

THOMAS BARBER.

And Vittellesco, he that was last General,
Being now turn'd cook to the Society,     45
Has dressed His Excellence such a dish of eggs—

PENNYBOY JUNIOR.

What, poach'd?

THOMAS BARBER.    No, powder'd.

CYMBAL.                 All the yolk is wildfire,

As he shall need beleaguer no more towns
But throw his egg in.

FITTON.             It shall clear consume
Palace and place, demolish and bear down     50
All strengths before it.

---

39. engineers] *F3;* Enginers *F.*     46.] *F margin: "His* Egges."

---

39. *engineers*] punning on *engineers* as (1) plotters and schemers and (2) inventors of machines used in warfare.

41–57.] Although these passages are clearly nonsense, the inventions attempted during the warfare of the early years of the century on the continent seem almost as preposterous: e.g., a gigantic chariot containing a movable fort, a floating battery that would rest on the bottom at low tide and rise with the flood. Spinola himself had a great reputation for the use of such devices. In *Volpone* (1605), II.i.51, Sir Politic Would-be identifies an imaginary war machine as "Spinola's whale."

44. *Vittellesco*] Mutius Vitelleschi, general of the Society of Jesus from 1615 to 1645, under whose leadership the Jesuits grew greatly in numbers, wealth, and influence.

46. *His Excellence*] Spinola.

46–52. *eggs . . . ruin*] These *powder'd* eggs (eggs filled with gun powder), whose *yolks* are *wildfire* (a composition of chemicals and gunpowder that was very hard to quench once it was ignited), were

CYMBAL.                    Never be extinguish'd
Till all become one ruin.
FITTON.                         And from Florence—
THOMAS BARBER.
They write was found in Galileo's study,
A burning glass (which they have sent him too)
To fire any fleet that's out at sea—                                    55
CYMBAL.
By moonshine, is't not so?
THOMAS BARBER.               Yes, sir, i'the water.
PENNYBOY JUNIOR.
His strengths will be unresistible if this hold!
Ha' you no news against him, on the contrary?
NATHANIEL.
Yes, sir. They write here one Cornelius-Son
Hath made the Hollanders an invisible eel                              60
To swim the haven at Dunkirk and sink all
The shipping there.
PENNYBOY JUNIOR.        Why ha' not you this, Tom?
CYMBAL.
Because he keeps the Pontifical side.
PENNYBOY JUNIOR.
How? Change sides, Tom. 'Twas never in my thought
To put thee up against ourselves. Come down                           65
Quickly.

54.] *F margin: "Galilaeo's study."*          59–60.] *F prints in margin: "The*
56–58.] *F margin: "The burning*          *Holanders Eele."*
*glasse, by Moon-shine."*          63. he] *F;* be *F3.*
59. S.P.] *Gifford;* Cla. *throughout*          64–66.] *F margin: "Peny-boy will*
*scene in F and F3.*          *haue him change sides:".*
59. sir] *F3;* Sit, *F.*

---

to be used as a substitute for the usual Spinola strategem whereby
he would *beleaguer* (lay seige to) important towns (e.g., Ostend,
Bergen op Zoom, Breda). Among the specialists employed by Spinola
were pyrotechnists (specialists in making gunpowder, wildfire, and
firearms).
    59. *Cornelius-Son*] Dutch "Cornelissen," Cornelius Drebbel, who
constructed a vessel in which he went from Westminster to Green-
wich with the boat partly submerged and his head above the surface
(H.S.).

CYMBAL.    Why, sir?

PENNYBOY JUNIOR.    I ventur'd not my money
    Upon those terms. If he may change, why so.
    I'll ha' him keep his own side, sure.

FITTON.                              Why, let him.
    'Tis but writing so much over again.

PENNYBOY JUNIOR.
    For that I'll bear the charge. There's two pieces.    70

FITTON.
    Come, do not stick with the gentleman.

CYMBAL.                          I'll take none, sir.
    And yet he shall ha' the place.

PENNYBOY JUNIOR.              They shall be ten then.
    Up, Tom, and th'Office shall take 'em. Keep your side, Tom.
                    [Tom changes sides with Nathaniel.]
    Know your own side. Do not forsake your side, Tom.

CYMBAL.
    Read.

THOMAS BARBER.    They write here, one Cornelius-Son    75
    Hath made the Hollanders an invisible eel
    To swim the haven at Dunkirk and sink all
    The shipping there.

PENNYBOY JUNIOR.        But how is't done?

CYMBAL.                          I'll show you, sir.
    It is an automa runs under water,
    With a snug nose, and has a nimble tail    80
    Made like an auger, with which tail she wriggles
    Betwixt the coasts of a ship and sinks it straight.

PENNYBOY JUNIOR.
    Whence ha' you this news?

FITTON.                      From a right hand I assure you,

73.] F margin: "though hee pay    78. sir.] F3; Sit. F.
for it."

---

79. automa] erroneous form of automaton.
80. snug] OED queries "snub"; H.S. suggest a connection with the
noun "snug," a rugged projection, a hard knob.
80. nimble tail] a propeller.
82. coasts] ribs.

  The eel boats here that lie before Queenhithe,
  Came out of Holland.

FITTON.         A most brave device   85
  To murder their flat bottoms.

FITTON.         I do grant you.
  But what if Spinola have a new project:
  To bring an army over in cork shoes
  And land them here at Harwich? All his horse
  Are shod with cork, and fourscore pieces of ordnance,  90
  Mounted upon cork carriages, with bladders
  Instead of wheels, to run the passage over
  At a spring tide.

PENNYBOY JUNIOR.  Is't true?

FITTON.       As true as the rest.

PENNYBOY JUNIOR.
  He'll never leave his engines. I would hear now
  Some curious news.

CYMBAL.   As what?

PENNYBOY JUNIOR.     Magic or alchemy  95
  Or flying i'the air, I care not what.

NATHANIEL.
  They write from Leipzig (reverence to your ears)
  The art of drawing farts out of dead bodies
  Is by the Brotherhood of the Rosy Cross
  Produc'd unto perfection in so sweet    100
  And rich a tincture—

FITTON.      As there is no princess
  But may perfume her chamber with th'extraction.

PENNYBOY JUNIOR.
  There's for you, princess.

87–89.] *F margin: "Spinola's new*  99.] *F margin: "Extraction of*
*proiect: an army in corkshooes."*  *farts."*

---

 84. *Queenhithe*] a quay on the northern bank of the Thames, near
Brook's Wharf, where the Dutch ships moored during Lent.

 95. *curious news*] news of the occult.

 98.] a proverbial symbol of an impossible task: "As soon may you
get a fart out of a dead man" (Tilley, F 63).

 99. *Brotherhood . . . Cross*] German followers of Christian Rosen-
kreuz.

PENNYBOY CANTER.          What, a fart for her?
PENNYBOY JUNIOR.
  I mean the spirit.
PENNYBOY CANTER.    Beware how she resents it.
PENNYBOY JUNIOR.
  And what hast thou, Tom?
THOMAS BARBER.               The perpetual motion          105
  Is here found out by an alewife in St. Katherine's,
  At the sign o'the Dancing Bears.
PENNYBOY JUNIOR.          What, from her tap?
  I'll go see that or else I'll send old Canter.
  He can make that discovery.
PENNYBOY CANTER.          Yes, in ale. [*Noise without.*]
PENNYBOY JUNIOR.
  Let me have all this news made up and seal'd.          110
REGISTER.
  The people press upon us. Please you, sir,
  Withdraw with your fair princess. There's a room
  Within, sir, to retire to.    *The* Register *offers him a room.*
PENNYBOY JUNIOR.          No, good Register,
  We'll stand it out here and observe your Office,
  What news it issues.
REGISTER.               'Tis the house of fame, sir,          115
  Where both the curious and the negligent,
  The scrupulous and careless, wild and staid,
  The idle and laborious, all do meet,
  To taste the *cornu copiae* of her rumors,
  Which she, the mother of sport, pleaseth to scatter          120
  Among the vulgar. Baits, sir, for the people!
  And they will bite like fishes.

104–105.] *F margin: "The per-*
*petuall Motion."*
109. S.D.] *Gifford.*
113. to retire to] *1716;* to retyre
too *F;* to retire too *F3.*

114–16.] *F margin: "The* Office
*call'd the house of fame."*
117. staid] *this edn.;* stay'd *F, F3.*

106–107. *alewife . . . Bears*] The lady whose inn bears this sign
appears in the *Masque of Augurs,* ll. 115 ff.
115. *house of fame*] As in Chaucer's *House of Fame, fame* means
rumor.

[*Enter three* Customers, *the first*] *a she* [*Ana*]*baptist.*

PENNYBOY JUNIOR.                    Let's see't.
CUSTOMER 1.
    Ha' you in your profane shop any news
    O'the saints at Amsterdam?
REGISTER.                    Yes, how much would you?
CUSTOMER 1.
    Six penny worth.
REGISTER.                Lay your money down. Read, Thomas.    125
THOMAS BARBER.
    The saints do write they expect a prophet shortly,
    The prophet Baal, to be sent over to them
    To calculate a time and half a time
    And the whole time, according to Naometry.
PENNYBOY JUNIOR.
    What's that?
THOMAS BARBER.    The measuring o'the Temple, a cabal        130
    Found out but lately and set out by Archie,
    Or some such head, of whose long coat they have heard,
    And being black, desire it.

---

123. S.P.] Dop. *throughout scene in F, F3.*
123–24.] *F margin:* I. *Cust. A she baptist.* H.S. suggest *"she* Anbaptist *F originally: she* baptist *F later, owing to derangement."*
127–29.] *F margin: "Prophet* Baal *expected in Holland."*
132–34.] *F margin: "* Archie *mourn'd then."*

---

123. S.P.] *F* reads Dop. for Dopper, from the Dutch *dooper,* a dipper, a Dutch baptist or anabaptist.

127. *Baal*] a pun on (1) the name given to a number of heathen fertility gods abhorred by the Old Testament prophets and (2) John Ball, a tailor who lent out money to be repaid "when King James should be crowned in the Pope's chaire" (Gifford).

128–29. *a time . . . time*] the period in which the woman was nourished in the wilderness away from the face of the serpent (Revelation 12:14).

129. *Naometry*] the system described in a work entitled *Naometria,* by the German mystic Simon Studion, in which the Second Coming is described when "that man of sin, the Pope" and "his son of perdition 'Mahomet' are overthrown" (H.S.).

131. *Archie*] Archie Armstrong, court fool to James I and Charles. He wore mourning for the death of James.

CUSTOMER 1.                    Peace be with them!
REGISTER.
    So there had need, for they are still by the ears
    One with another.
CUSTOMER 1.                    It is their zeal.
REGISTER.                        Most likely.                    135
CUSTOMER 1.
    Have you no other of that species?
REGISTER.                            Yes,
    But dearer, it will cost you a shilling.
CUSTOMER 1.                            Verily,
    There is a nine-pence, I will shed no more.
REGISTER.
    Not to the good o'the saints?
CUSTOMER 1.                        I am not sure
    That man is good.
REGISTER.                    Read, from Constantinople,          140
    Nine penny'orth.
THOMAS BARBER.        They give out here, the grand Signor
    Is certainly turn'd Christian, and to clear
    The controversy 'twixt the Pope and him,
    Which is the Antichrist, he means to visit
    The Church at Amsterdam this very summer          145
    And quit all marks o'the beast.
CUSTOMER 1.                    Now joyful tidings.
 · Who brought in this? Which emissary?
REGISTER.                            Buz,
    Your countryman.
CUSTOMER 1.            Now, blessed be the man
    And his whole family, with the nation.
REGISTER.
    Yes, for Amboyna, and the justice there.          150

141–42.] *F margin: "The great*
Turk *turn'd* Christian."

---

  141. *grand Signor*] Sultan of Turkey.
  146. *marks . . . beast*] the marks on evil men referred to in Revelation 16:2 and 19:20.
  150. *Amboyna . . . justice there*] a reference to the Massacre of Amboyna (1623), in which the Dutch tortured and killed a party of

This is a Dopper, a she Anabaptist.
Seal and deliver her her news, dispatch.

CUSTOMER 2.

Ha' you any news from the Indies? Any miracle
Done in Japan by the Jesuits, or in China?

NATHANIEL.

No, but we hear of a colony of cooks                      155
To be set ashore o'the coast of America
For the conversion of the cannibals
And making them good, eating Christians.
Here comes the colonel that undertakes it.

[*Enter* Lickfinger.]

CUSTOMER 3.

Who? Captain Lickfinger?

LICKFINGER.                           News, news my boys!    160
I am to furnish a great feast today,
And I would have what news the Office affords.

NATHANIEL.

We were venting some of you, of your new project,

REGISTER.

Afore 'twas paid for. You were somewhat too hasty.

PENNYBOY JUNIOR.

What, Lickfinger, wilt thou convert the cannibals          165
With spit and pan divinity?

---

153.] *F margin: "2. Cust."*
155–59.] *F margin: "A* Coloney *oe*
Cookes *sent ouer to conuert the*
Canniballs."
158. Christians] *F3;* Cbristians *F.*

160. S.P. CUSTOMER 3] *F3;* C.2. *F.*
*F margin: "3 Cust."*
161–62.] *F margin: "By* Colonel
Lickfinger."

---

Englishmen at an East India Company trading post as part of a
successful attempt to wrest control of the Spice Islands from the
British. Long afterwards, reminders of this incident were used to
inflame the passions of Englishmen against the Dutch (e.g., Dryden's
tragedy of *Amboyna* [1673], written during the Third Dutch War).

159. *colonel*] trisyllabic at this date.

165–80. *wilt . . . there*] This passage parallels the accomplishments
the comic poet Athenion attributes to cooks in Athenaeus *Deipno-
sophistae* 14. 660e–661d.

LICKFINGER.                          Sir, for that
I will not urge but for the fire and zeal
To the true cause. Thus I have undertaken;
With two lay brethren to myself, no more,
One o'the broach, th'other o'the boiler,                    170
In one six months, and by plain cookery,
No magic to't, but old Japet's physic,
The father of the European arts,
To make such sauces for the savages,
And cook their meats, with those enticing steams,          175
As it would make our cannibal-Christians
Forbear the mutual eating one another,
Which they do do more cunningly than the wild
Anthropophagi, that snatch only strangers,
Like my old patron's dogs there.

PENNYBOY JUNIOR.                     Oh, my uncle's.        180
Is dinner ready, Lickfinger?

LICKFINGER.                          When you please, sir.
I was bespeaking but a parcel of news
To strew out the long meal withal, but 't seems
You are furnish'd here already.

PENNYBOY JUNIOR.                     Oh, not half!

LICKFINGER.
What court news is there? Any proclamations               185
Or edicts to come forth?

THOMAS BARBER.                   Yes, there is one,
That the king's barber has got, for aid of our trade,
Whereof there is a manifest decay,
A precept for the wearing of long hair,
To run to seed, to sow bald pates withal,                 190

---

174. To] *F;* Yo *F3.*              189–92.] *F margin: "To let long*
175. cook] *1716;* cookes *F;* Cooks   *hayre runne to seed, to sow bald*
*F3.*                                *pates."*

---

170. *broach*] spit.
172. *Japet's physic*] In fact it was Japetus' son Prometheus who
brought down fire from heaven.
179. *Anthropophagi*] race of man-eaters.
183. *To strew . . . withal*] to intersperse with the meal.

And the preserving fruitful heads and chins
To help a mystery almost antiquated.
Such as are bald and barren beyond hope
Are to be separated, and set by
For ushers to old countesses.

LICKFINGER.                     And coachmen,          195
To mount their boxes reverently and drive,
Like lapwings, with a shell upo' their heads,
Through the streets. Ha' you no news o'the stage?
They'll ask me about new plays at dinner time,
And I should be as dumb as a fish.

THOMAS BARBER.                  Oh, yes.          200
There is a legacy left to the King's Players,
Both for their various shifting of their scene
And dext'rous change o'their persons to all shapes
And all disguises, by the right reverend
Archbishop of Spalato.

LICKFINGER.             He is dead          205
That play'd him!

THOMAS BARBER.     Then h'has lost his share o'the legacy.

LICKFINGER.

What news of Gondomar?

199. about] *F3;* abou *F.*          201–3.] *F margin:* "Spalato's *Leg-*
                                     *acy to the* Players."

---

192. *mystery*] craft.

195–98. *And coachmen . . . streets*] This proverbial simile is used
to criticize the fashionable practice of having coachmen ride bare-
headed. "Like a lapwing that runs away with the shell on its head"
(Tilley, L 69).

201. *King's Players*] the King's Men or His Majesty's Players, who
also presented *The Staple of News.*

202. *scene*] scene or location, not scenery.

205. *Archbishop of Spalato*] Marc Antonio de Dominis, Archbishop
of Spalatro, sought to establish a Universal Church. He went to
England in 1616, where he was at first rewarded and encouraged by
King James. He was, however, forced to flee in 1622 and went to
Rome, where he escaped the Inquisition for a year, enjoying the
protection of his friend Pope Gregory XV (1621–23).

205–6. *He . . . him!*] William Rowley, who had played the Fat
Bishop, a satire on de Dominis, in Middleton's *A Game at Chess,* 1624.

207. *Gondomar*] Diego Sarmiento d'Acuña, Count of Gondomar,
Spanish diplomat who worked toward peace and a royal wedding

THOMAS BARBER.                    A second fistula
  Or an excoriation (at the least)
  For putting the poor English play was writ of him
  To such a sordid use, as (is said) he did,                210
  Of cleansing his posteriors.
LICKFINGER.                       Justice! Justice!
THOMAS BARBER.
  Since when, he lives condemn'd to his chair at Brussels,
  And there sits filing certain politic hinges
  To hang the States on h'has heav'd off the hooks.
LICKFINGER.
  What must you have for these?
PENNYBOY JUNIOR.            Thou shalt pay nothing, 215
  But reckon 'em in i'the bill.          [*Exit* Lickfinger.]
                              There's twenty pieces
  Her grace bestows upon the Office, Tom.

  *He gives twenty pieces to* [Cymbal *for*] *the Office.*

  Write thou that down for news.
REGISTER.                      We may well do't;
  We have not many such.
PENNYBOY JUNIOR.         There's twenty more
  If you say so.                      *Doubles it.*
        My princess is a princess!                    220
  And put that too under the Office seal.

208. the least] F; least F3              212. chair] *de Winter;* share F, F3.
208–13.] F *margin:* "Gundomar's     216. in i'the] F; 'i the F3.
*vse of the game at* Chesse, *or* Play
*so called.*"

---

between England and Spain, and tried to make England an ally of
the Catholic powers in the conflict that led to the Thirty Years War.
He is satirized as the Black Knight in *A Game at Chess.*
  209. *poor English play*] Jonson also expressed contempt for Middleton in *Conversations with Drummond*, 1. 168. *A Game at Chess* was
extraordinarily popular and profitable but was suppressed at Gondomar's insistence on the grounds that it represented living Christian
kings on the stage. (The White King is King James I; the Black
King is Philip IV of Spain.)
  212. *chair*] The special furniture required to accommodate the
famous fistula is referred to in the S.D. at the beginning of Act V
of Middleton's play.

Cymbal *takes* Pecunia *aside, courts and wooes her to the Office.*
[Fitton *courts the* Waitingwomen.]

CYMBAL.

> If it will please your grace to sojourn here
> And take my roof for covert, you shall know
> The rites belonging to your blood and birth,
> Which few can apprehend. These sordid servants,          225
> Which rather are your keepers than attendants,
> Should not come near your presence. I would have
> You waited on by ladies, and your train
> Borne up by persons of quality and honor.
> Your meat should be serv'd in with curious dances          230
> And set upon the board with virgin hands
> Tun'd to their voices, not a dish remov'd
> But to the music, nor a drop of wine
> Mix'd with his water without harmony.

PECUNIA.

> You are a courtier, sir, or somewhat more,          235
> That have this tempting language.

CYMBAL.                              I'm your servant,
> Excellent princess, and would ha' you appear
> That which you are. Come forth, the state and wonder
> Of these our times, dazzle the vulgar eyes
> And strike the people blind with admiration.          240

PENNYBOY CANTER [*aside*].

> Why, that's the end of wealth! Thrust riches outward
> And remain beggars within: contemplate nothing
> But the vile sordid things of time, place, money,
> And let the noble and the precious go.
> Virtue and honesty, hang 'em, poor thin membranes          245
> Of honor. Who respects them? Oh, the Fates!

238. the state] *Whalley;* State, *F,*
*F3.*

---

234. *his*] its.
238. *state*] splendor.
239–48. *dazzle . . . any!*] This passage is a versification of the translation of Seneca's *Epistles* 115 and 119, which Jonson had included in
*Timber,* ll. 1375–80 and 1448–49.

How hath all just, true reputation fall'n
Since money, this base money 'gan to have any!

Fitton *hath been courting the* Waitingwomen *this while, and is
jeered by them.*

BAND.

Pity the gentleman is not immortal—

WAX.

As he gives out the place is by description.                    250

FITTON.

A very paradise if you saw all, lady.

WAX.

I am the chambermaid, sir, you mistake,
My lady may see all.

FITTON.

Sweet Mistress Statute, gentle Mistress Band,
And Mother Mortgage, do but get her grace                    255
To sojourn here.

PICKLOCK.                    I thank you, gentle Wax.

MORTGAGE.

If it were a chattel, I would try my credit.

PICKLOCK.

So it is, for term of life, we count it so.

STATUTE.

She means inheritance to him and his heirs,
Or that he could assure a state of years;                    260
I'll be his Statute-Staple, Statute-Merchant,
Or what he please.

PICKLOCK.                    He can expect no more.

BAND.

His cousin, Alderman Security,
That he did talk of so e'en now—

STATUTE.                                        Who is
The very brooch o'the bench, gem o'the City—                    265

---

261. *Statute-Staple, Statute-Merchant*] bonds of record acknowledged
before the mayor of the Staple and the chief magistrate of a trading
town, respectively, that gave to the obligee power of seizure of the
land of the obligor if he failed to pay his debt at the appointed time.

BAND.

> He and his deputy but assure his life
> For one seven years.

STATUTE.                    And see what we'll do for him

> Upon his scarlet motion—

BAND.                    And old chain,

> That draws the City ears—

WAX.                    When he says nothing

> But twirls it thus.

STATUTE.          A moving oratory!                    270

BAND.

> Dumb rhetoric and silent eloquence,
> As the fine poet says.

FITTON.                    Come, they all scorn us.

> Do you not see't? The family of scorn!

BROKER.

> Do not believe him. Gentle Master Picklock,
> They understood you not. The gentlewomen,          275
> They thought you would ha' my lady sojourn with you,
> And you desire but now and then a visit.

PICKLOCK.

> Yes, if she pleas'd, sir, it would much advance
> Unto the Office, her continual residence.
> (I speak but as a member.)

BROKER.                    'Tis enough.                    280

> I apprehend you. And it shall go hard,
> But I'll so work as somebody shall work her.

PICKLOCK.

> Pray you change with our master but a word about it.

PENNYBOY JUNIOR.

> Well, Lickfinger, see that our meat be ready,
> Thou hast news enough.

---

268. *scarlet*] color of an alderman's robes.

268. *chain*] worn by an alderman on ceremonial occasions.

271–72. *Dumb . . . says*] Samuel Daniel, "Sweet silent rethorique of perswading eyes/ Dombe eloquence, whose powre doth moue the blood" (*The Complaint of Rosamond*, ll. 121–22).

273. *family of scorn*] as contrasted with the members of the mystical sect known as The Family of Love.

LICKFINGER. Something of Bethlem Gabor, 285
And then I'm gone.

THOMAS BARBER. We hear he has devis'd
A drum, to fill all Christendom with the sound,
But that he cannot draw his forces near it
To march yet, for the violence of the noise.
And therefore he is fain by a design 290
To carry 'em in the air, and at some distance,
Till he be married. Then they shall appear.

LICKFINGER.
Or never. Well, God b'wi'you! (Stay, who's here?)
A little of the Duke of Bavier, and then—

NATHANIEL.
H'has taken a gray habit and is turn'd 295
The church's miller, grinds the Catholic grist
With every wind, and Tilly takes the toll.

CUSTOMER 4.
Ha' you any news o'the pageants to send down
Into the several counties? All the country
Expected from the city most brave speeches, 300
Now, at the coronation.

LICKFINGER. It expected
More than it understood, for they stand mute,
Poor innocent dumb things. They are but wood,

287–88.] *F margin:* "Bethlem Ga- 298.] *F margin:* "4. *Cust.*"
bors *Drum.*" 298–99.] *F margin:* "*The Pag-*
294–95.] *F margin:* "*The* Duke *of eants.*"
Bauier."

---

285–92. *Bethlem . . . appear*] Bethlen Gabor, Prince of Transylvania,
a devout Calvinist with a large army, had sought the hand of the
Emperor Ferdinand's daughter in exchange for promising to lead his
troops against Ferdinand's enemy the Turks. When Ferdinand refused,
Bethlen sought the hand of Catherine, sister of the Elector of Branden-
burg, by promising help in fighting Ferdinand and the Catholic
League. His marriage to Catherine and his subsequent resumption of
fighting in the Protestant cause did not take place until after the play
was acted.

294. *Duke of Bavier*] Maximilian of Bavaria; see III.ii.32, note.

301. *Now . . . coronation*] The coronation of Charles I took place
on 2 February, 1626.

301–2. *expected . . . understood.*] See Induction, ll. 30–31, note.

As is the bench and blocks they were wrought on, yet
If May Day come and the sun shine, perhaps          305
They'll sing like Memnon's statue and be vocal.

CUSTOMER 5.

Ha' you any forest news?

THOMAS BARBER.                    None very wild, sir.
Some tame there is, out o'the forest of fools,
A new park is a-making there, to sever
Cuckolds of antler from the rascals. Such          310
Whose wives are dead, and have since cast their heads,
Shall remain cuckolds pollard.

LICKFINGER.                    I'll ha' that news.

CUSTOMER 1.
And I.

CUSTOMER 2.    And I.

CUSTOMER 3.        And I.

CUSTOMER 4            And I.

CUSTOMER 5.                    And I.

Pennyboy [Junior] *would invite the Master of the Office.*

CYMBAL.

Sir, I desire to be excus'd, and madam,
I cannot leave my office the first day.          315
My cousin Fitton here shall wait upon you,
And emissary Picklock.

PENNYBOY JUNIOR.          And Tom *Clericus?*

CYMBAL.

I cannot spare him yet, but he shall follow you
When they have ordered the rolls. Shut up th'office,
When you ha' done, till two o'clock.          320
                    [*Exeunt all but* Tom *and* Nathaniel.]

307.] *F margin:* "5. *Cust.*"          308–11.] *F margin:* "*The new*
                              Parke *in the* Forrest *of* Fooles."

---

306. *Memnon's statue*] Memnon's name was connected with a statue
of Amenhotep III near Thebes; after an earthquake when part of the
statue fell, whenever the rays of the sun touched the statue, it made
a noise like the twang of a harp string.
310. *rascals*] young, lean, or inferior deer.
311. *heads*] antlers.
312. *pollard*] without horns.

[III.iii]      [*Enter*] Shunfield, Almanac, Madrigal.

SHUNFIELD.
By your leave, clerks,
Where shall we dine today? Do you know?

TIIOMAS BARBER.                              The jeerers!

ALMANAC.
Where's my fellow Fitton?

THOMAS BARBER.              New gone forth.

SHUNFIELD.
Cannot your Office tell us what brave fellows
Do eat together today in town, and where?                    5

THOMAS BARBER.
Yes, there's a gentleman, the brave heir, young Pennyboy,
Dines in Apollo.

MADRIGAL.              Come let's thither then.
I ha' supp'd in Apollo.

ALMANAC.              With the Muses?

MADRIGAL.                              No,
But with two gentlewomen call'd the Graces.

ALMANAC.
They were ever three in poetry.

MADRIGAL.                    This was truth, sir.        10

THOMAS BARBER.
Sir, Master Fitton's there, too.

SHUNFIELD.              All the better.

ALMANAC.
We may have a jeer, perhaps.

SHUNFIELD.                    Yes, you'll drink, doctor,
(If there be any good meat) as much good wine now
As would lay up a Dutch Ambassador.

THOMAS BARBER.
If he dine there, he's sure to have good meat,          15
For Lickfinger provides the dinner.

ALMANAC.                    Who?
The glory o'the kitchen, that holds cookery
A trade from Adam, quotes his broths and salads,

---

0.1.] Shunfield, Almanac, Madrigal, Clerks. *F, F3.*
2. S.P.] *H.S.;* Nath. *Gifford, who*

*also suggests the possible attribu-
tion of the lines to Tho. Barber;
F and F3 give ll. 1–2 to Shunfield.*

And swears he's not dead yet, but translated
In some immortal crust, the paste of almonds?                    20
MADRIGAL.
    The same.  He holds no man can be a poet
    That is not a good cook, to know the palates
    And several tastes o'the time.  He draws all arts
    Out of the kitchen but the art of poetry,
    Which he concludes the same with cookery.                    25
SHUNFIELD.
    Tut, he maintains more heresies than that.
    He'll draw the magisterium from a minc'd pie,
    And prefer jellies to your juleps, doctor.
ALMANAC.
    I was at an olla podrida of his making,
    Was a brave piece of cookery, at a funeral.                  30
    But opening the pot-lid, he made us laugh
    Who had wept all day, and sent us such a tickling
    Into our nostrils as the funeral feast
    Had been a wedding dinner.
SHUNFIELD.                          Gi' him allowance,
    And that but moderate, he will make a Siren                  35
    Sing i'the kettle, send in an Arion,
    In a brave broth and of a wat'ry green
    Just the sea color, mounted on the back
    Of a grown conger but in such a posture
    As all the world would take him for a dolphin.               40
MADRIGAL.
    He's a rare fellow, without question.  But
    He holds some paradoxes.

---

23–25. *He . . . cookery*] Cooking occupies the same exalted position in *Neptune's Triumph*, ll. 85–86.

27. *magisterium*] philosopher's stone.

27. *minc'd pie*] not the modern dessert but a substantial baked meat of minced flesh, fowl, or fish.

28. *juleps*] sweet drinks used as vehicles for medicines.

29. *olla podrida*] dish of Portuguese origin composed of many kinds of flesh, fowl, and small birds stewed or boiled together, served over pieces of bread, and covered with stewed dried fruit and slices of oranges and lemons (Markham, pp. 74–75).

35–40. *he . . . dolphin*] Except that the Cook's device had twenty Sirens, this speech echoes *Neptune's Triumph*, ll. 185–91.

ALMANAC.                         Ay, and pseudodoxes.
  Marry, for most he's orthodox i'the kitchen.
MADRIGAL.
  And knows the clergy's taste.
ALMANAC.                         Ay, and the laity's.
SHUNFIELD.
  You think not o' your time. We'll come too late          45
  If we go not presently.
MADRIGAL.                   Away then.
SHUNFIELD.                             Sirs.
  You must get o' this news to store your office:
  Who dines and sups i'the town, where, and with whom.
  'Twill be beneficial. When you are stor'd
  And as we like our fare, we shall reward you.            50
NATHANIEL.
  A hungry trade 'twill be.
THOMAS BARBER.            Much like Duke Humphrey's,
  But now and then, as th' wholesome proverb says,
  'Twill *obsonare famem ambulando.*
NATHANIEL.
  Shut up the office, gentle brother Thomas.
THOMAS BARBER.
  Brother Nathaniel, I ha' the wine for you.               55
  I hope to see us, one day, emissaries.
NATHANIEL.
  Why not? 'Slid, I despair not to be Master!   [*Exeunt.*]


51. S.P.] *Gifford; Cla. here and at
ll. 54 and 57 in F and F3.*

---

  43. *Marry*] why, to be sure.
  51. *Duke Humphrey's*] proverbial: "To dine with Duke Humphrey"
meaning to go hungry (Tilley, D 63); Stow explains the source of the
expression as the custom of dinnerless gallants who spent the dinner
hour in Duke Humphrey's Walk at St. Paul's (1:335).
  53. *obsonare famem ambulando*] to provide an appetite by walking
(Cicero *Tusculan Disputations* 5. 97).
  55. *I ha' . . . you*] Gifford says it is a proverbial expression meaning
"I have the perquisites [of the office] which you are to share."
  57. *'Slid*] by God's eyelid.

[III.iv]

  [*Enter*] Pennyboy Senior [*and*] Broker [*at different doors*].

PENNYBOY SENIOR.

　　How now?　　　　　　*He is started with Broker's coming back.*
　　　　　　I think I was born under Hercules' star!
　　Nothing but trouble and tumult to oppress me.
　　Why come you back? Where is your charge?

BROKER.　　　　　　　　　　　　　　　　I ha' brought
　　A gentleman to speak with you.

PENNYBOY SENIOR.　　　　　　　　To speak with me?
　　You know 'tis death for me to speak with any man.　　　　5
　　What is he? Set me a chair.

BROKER.　　　　　　　　　　　　He's the Master
　　Of the great Office.

PENNYBOY SENIOR.　　　What?

BROKER.　　　　　　　　　　　The Staple of News,
　　A mighty thing. They talk six thousand a year.

PENNYBOY SENIOR.
　　Well, bring your six in. Where ha' you left Pecunia?

BROKER.
　　Sir, in Apollo. They are scarce set.

PENNYBOY SENIOR.　　　　　　　　　Bring six.　　　　10

　　　　[Broker *exits and returns with* Cymbal.]

BROKER.
　　Here is the gentleman.

PENNYBOY SENIOR.　　　　　He must pardon me.
　　I cannot rise, a diseas'd man.

CYMBAL.　　　　　　　　　　By no means, sir.
　　Respect your health and ease.

PENNYBOY SENIOR.　　　　　　It is no pride in me,
　　But pain, pain. What's your errand, sir, to me?
　　Broker, return to your charge. Be Argus-eyed,　　　15

0.1. *Enter . . . doors.*] *Gifford;*
Pennyboy Senior, Broker, Cymbal.
*F, F3.*

————————————————————————

　1. S.D. *started*] startled.

Awake to the affair you have in hand.
Serve in Apollo but take heed of Bacchus.
                                        *He sends* Broker *back.*
Go on, sir.
CYMBAL.            I am come to speak with you.
PENNYBOY SENIOR.
'Tis pain for me to speak, a very death,
But I will hear you.
CYMBAL.                        Sir, you have a lady,            20
That sojourns with you.
PENNYBOY SENIOR.            Ha! I am somewhat short
In my sense too—            *He pretends infirmity.*
CYMBAL.            Pecunia.
PENNYBOY SENIOR.            O'that side,
Very imperfect on—
CYMBAL.                        Whom I would draw
Oft'ner to a poor office I am Master of—
PENNYBOY SENIOR.
My hearing is very dead. You must speak quicker.    25
CYMBAL.
Or, if it please you, sir, to let her sojourn
In part with me, I have a moiety
We will divide, half of the profits.
PENNYBOY SENIOR.                        Ha!
I hear you better now. How come they in?
Is it a certain business or a casual?                30
For I am loath to seek out doubtful courses,
Run any hazardous paths. I love straight ways,
A just and upright man! Now all trade totters.
The trade of money is fall'n two i'the hundred.
That was a certain trade while th'age was thrifty    35
And men good husbands, look'd unto their stocks,
Had their minds bounded. Now the public riot
Prostitutes all, scatters away in coaches,
In footmen's coats, and waitingwomen's gowns.
                        *He talks vehemently and aloud.*
They must have velvet haunches (with a pox)          40

---

36. *husbands*] managers of their own affairs or business.

Now taken up and yet not pay the use.
Bate of the use! I am mad with this time's manners.

CYMBAL.

You said e'en now it was death for you to speak.

PENNYBOY SENIOR.

Ay, but an anger, a just anger (as this is)
Puts life in man. Who can endure to see          45
The fury of men's gullets and their groins?
What fires, what cooks, what kitchens might be spar'd?
                    *Is mov'd more and more.*
What stews, ponds, parks, coops, garners, magazines,
What velvets, tissues, scarfs, embroideries,
And laces they might lack? They covet things          50
Superfluous still, when it were much more honor
They could want necessary. What need hath Nature
Of silver dishes or gold chamber pots,
Of perfum'd napkins or a numerous family
To see her eat? Poor and wise, she requires          55
Meat only. Hunger is not ambitious.
Say that you were the emperor of pleasures,
The great dictator of fashions for all Europe,
And had the pomp of all the courts and kingdoms
Laid forth unto the show to make yourself          60
Gaz'd and admir'd at? You must go to bed
And take your natural rest; then all this vanisheth.
Your bravery was but shown; 'twas not possess'd.
While it did boast itself it was then perishing.

CYMBAL [*aside*].

This man has healthful lungs.

---

47. kitchens] *F3;* kitckins *F.*

---

41. *taken up*] borrowed.
41. *use*] interest.
45–68. *Who . . . lives*] in large part a versification of Jonson's translation of Seneca's *Epistles* 110 and 119, which appears in *Timber,* ll. 1387–412.
48. *stews*] ponds in which fish were kept for the table.
49. *tissues*] fine cloth often interwoven with gold or silver.
54. *napkins*] handkerchiefs.
61. *admir'd*] wondered.

PENNYBOY SENIOR.                    All that excess                    65
    Appear'd as little yours as the spectators'.
    It scarce fills up the expectation
    Of a few hours that entertains men's lives.
CYMBAL [aside].
    He has the monopoly of sole-speaking.

               [To Pennyboy Senior.]

    Why, good sir, you talk all.                    70
PENNYBOY SENIOR.                    Why should I not?    He is angry.
    Is it not under mine own roof, my ceiling?
CYMBAL.
    But I came here to talk with you.
PENNYBOY SENIOR.                    Why, an' I will not
    Talk with you, sir? You are answer'd. Who sent for you?
CYMBAL.
    Nobody sent for me—
PENNYBOY SENIOR.                    But you came. Why then
    Go as you came. Here's no man holds you. There,    75
    There lies your way. You see the door.
CYMBAL.                    This's strange!
PENNYBOY SENIOR.
    'Tis my civility when I do not relish
    The party or his business. Pray you be gone, sir.
    I'll ha' no venture in your ship, the Office,
    Your bark of six, if 'twere sixteen, good sir.        80
CYMBAL.
    You are a rogue!
PENNYBOY SENIOR.    I think I am, sir, truly.
CYMBAL.
    A rascal and a money-bawd!
PENNYBOY SENIOR.                    My surnames.
CYMBAL.
    A wretched rascal!
PENNYBOY SENIOR.        You will overflow—
    And spill all.

---

72. here] F3; hete F.      81–83.] F margin: "Cymbal railes
73–75.] F margin: "Bids him get    at him."
out of his house."

CYMBAL.                    Caterpillar, moth,
  Horse leech, and dung worm—
PENNYBOY SENIOR.                    Still you lose your labor.    85
  I am a broken vessel—all runs out—
  A shrunk old dry-fat. Fare you well, good six!    [*Exeunt.*]

## THE THIRD INTERMEAN AFTER THE THIRD ACT

CENSURE.
  A notable tough rascal, this old Pennyboy, right City-
bred!
MIRTH.
  In Silver Street, the region of money, a good seat for a
usurer.
TATTLE.
  He has rich ingredients in him, I warrant you, if they    5
were extracted. A true receipt to make an alderman an'
he were well wrought upon, according to art.
EXPECTATION.
  I would fain see an alderman in chimia, that is, a treatise
of aldermanity truly written.
CENSURE.
  To show how much it differs from urbanity.    10
MIRTH.
  Ay, or humanity. Either would appear in this Pennyboy,
an' he were rightly distill'd. But how like you the news?
You are gone from that.
CENSURE.
  Oh, they are monstrous, scurvy, and stale! And too
exotic, ill cook'd, and ill dish'd!    15

[III.iv]                              [III.Intermean]
84–85.] F *margin: "He ieeres him."*    3. a] F; an F3.

---

3. *Silver Street*] London Street running west from Wood Street; Stow
derives its name from the silversmiths living there (1: 299).
  8. *chimia*] second component of the Arabic word from which
*alchemy* is adapted: *al,* = the; *chimia,* = Egyptian art.
  9. *aldermanity*] nonce word meaning having the quality of an alderman.
  15. *exotic*] outlandish.

EXPECTATION.

They were as good yet as butter could make them.

TATTLE.

In a word, they were beastly buttered! He shall never
come o' my bread more, nor in my mouth, if I can help
it. I have had better news from the bake-house by ten
thousand parts, in a morning, or the conduits in West-   20
minster: all the news of Tuttle Street and both the
Alm'ries, the two Sanctuaries, long and round Wool-
staple, with King's Street and Cannon Row to boot!

MIRTH.

Ay, my gossip Tattle knew what fine slips grew in
Gardener's Lane, who kiss'd the butcher's wife with the   25
cow's breath, what matches were made in the Bowling
Alley, and what bets won and lost; how much grist went

17. He] *F;* she *F3.*                    19. have had] *F;* have *F3.*
18. in my] *F3;* my in *F.*

---

19–20. *bake-house . . . conduits*] traditional gathering places for gossips.
    20. *conduits*] fountains that supplied water for the city before pipes
carried it directly to the houses.
    21–29. *Tuttle . . . Fields*] all places mentioned in this passage are
in Westminster.
    21. *Tuttle Street*] Tothill Street, running west from the Broad or
Great Sanctuary to Broadway.
    21–22. *both the Alm'ries*] Great and Little Almonries, almshouses
for poor men and women, west of Westminster Abbey.
    22. *two Sanctuaries*] Great, or Broad, and Little Sanctuaries, pre-
cincts on the north and west sides of Westminster.
    22–23. *long . . . Woolstaple*] the two parts of the central Woolstaple
for England, north of New Palace Yard.
    23. *King's Street*] running from Charing Cross, London, to the
Palace of Westminster.
    23. *Cannon Row*] running into Bridge Street, east of Parliament
Street.
    24–25. *fine . . . Lane*] Gardener's Lane, running from King's Street
to Delahey Street. Sugden interprets this allusion to mean "what
illegitimate children were born there." The pun rather than the
reputation of the street prompted Jonson's choice.
    26–27. *Bowling Alley*] now Bowling Street, from Dean's Yard to
Tufton Street.

to the mill, and what besides; who conjur'd in Tuttle
Fields, and how many, when they never came there; and
which boy rode upon Doctor Lamb, in the likeness of a    30
roaring lion, that run away with him in his teeth and
has not devour'd him yet.

TATTLE.

Why, I had it from my maid Joan Hearsay, and she had
it from a limb o'the school, she says, a little limb of
nine-year old, who told her the master left out his      35
conjuring book one day and he found it, and so the
fable came about. But whether it were true or no, we
gossips are bound to believe it an't be once out and
afoot. How should we entertain the time else, or find
ourselves in fashionable discourse for all companies if we  40
do not credit all and make more of it in the reporting?

CENSURE.

For my part, I believe it. And there were no wiser than
I, I would have ne'er a cunning schoolmaster in England.
I mean a cunning man, a schoolmaster, that is a conjurer
or a poet or that had any acquaintance with a poet.      45
They make all their scholars playboys. Is't not a fine
sight to see all our children made interluders? Do we
pay our money for this? We send them to learn their
grammar and their Terence, and they learn their play-
books. Well, they talk we shall have no more Parlia-     50
ments (God bless us), but an' we have, I hope Zeal-

---

28–29. *Tuttle Fields*] Tothill Fields, a large piece of open land south
of Tuttle (Tothill) Street.

30. *Doctor Lamb*] See I.Intermean, l. 48, note.

44. *cunning man*] conjuror.

46. *scholars playboys*] refers to the Latin play put on each year by
the boys of Westminster School.

50–51. *they . . . Parliaments*] Charles I's brief initial Parliament
(18 June to 12 August 1625, including a two-week adjournment) had
been summarily dissolved when it became clear that Charles would
tolerate no criticism of his favorite Buckingham and the Parliament
would not vote him the subsidies he wanted. Since Charles felt he
had the right to call Parliament or not as he pleased and since he
was so greatly angered by the behavior of his first Parliament, there
were ample grounds for such a rumor.

of-the-Land Busy and my gossip Rabbi Trouble-Truth
will start up and see we shall have painful good
ministers to keep school and catechize our youth and not
teach 'em to speak plays and act fables of false news in      55
this manner, to the supervexation of town and country,
with a wanion.


[IV.i]
Pennyboy Junior, Fitton, Shunfield, Almanac, Madrigal, Pennyboy Canter, [and] Picklock [sitting at table].

PENNYBOY JUNIOR.
    Come, gentlemen, let's breathe from healths awhile.
    This Lickfinger has made us a good dinner
    For our Pecunia. What shall's do with ourselves
    While the women water and the fiddlers eat?
FITTON.
    Let's jeer a little.
PENNYBOY JUNIOR.        Jeer? What's that?
SHUNFIELD.                                    Expect, sir.      5
ALMANAC.
    We first begin with ourselves and then at you.
SHUNFIELD.
    A game we use.
MADRIGAL.              We jeer all kind of persons
    We meet withal, of any rank or quality;
    And if we cannot jeer them, we jeer ourselves.
PENNYBOY CANTER.
    A pretty sweet society, and a grateful!                    10
PICKLOCK.
    Pray, let's see some.


IV.i] F; Act. IV. Scene II. F3.

---

[III.Intermean]
    51–52. Zeal-of-the-Land Busy] a zealous and hypocritical Puritan in
Bartholomew Fair.
    53–54. good ministers] an allusion to the Puritan hatred of the stage.
    57. with a wanion] with a vengeance.

SHUNFIELD.                    Have at you then, lawyer.
They say there was one of your coat in Bedlam lately.
ALMANAC.
I wonder all his clients were not there.
MADRIGAL.
They were the madder sort.
PICKLOCK.                              Except, sir, one
Like you, and he made verses.
FITTON.                              Madrigal,                    15
A jeer.
MADRIGAL.    I know.
SHUNFIELD.        But what did you do, lawyer,
When you made love to Mistress Band at dinner?
MADRIGAL.
Why, of an advocate, he grew the client.
PENNYBOY JUNIOR.
Well play'd, my poet.
MADRIGAL.                    And show'd the law of nature
Was there above the common law.
SHUNFIELD.                              Quit, quit.                    20
PENNYBOY JUNIOR.
Call you this jeering? I can play at this.
'Tis like a ball at tennis.
FITTON.                              Very like.
But we were not well in.
ALMANAC.                              'Tis indeed, sir,
When we do speak at volley all the ill
We can one of another.
SHUNFIELD.                    As this morning                    25
(I would you had heard us) of the rogue your uncle.
ALMANAC.
That money-bawd.
MADRIGAL.                    We call'd him a coat-card
O'the last order.
PENNYBOY JUNIOR.    What's that? A knave?

---

12. Bedlam] St. Mary of Bethlehem's hospital in Bishopsgate, used
as a madhouse.
24. at volley] at random (Fr. à la volée).
27. coat-card] a playing card with a coated figure, a face card.

MADRIGAL.
    Some readings have it so. My manuscript
    Doth speak it, varlet.
PENNYBOY CANTER.          And yourself a fool                    30
    O'the first rank, and one shall have the leading
    O'the right-hand file under this brave commander.
PENNYBOY JUNIOR.
    What say'st thou, Canter?
PENNYBOY CANTER.          Sir, I say this is
    A very wholesome exercise and comely,
    Like lepers showing one another their scabs          35
    Or flies feeding on ulcers.
PENNYBOY JUNIOR.                What news, gentlemen?
    Ha' you any news for after dinner? Methinks
    We should not spend our time unprofitably.
PENNYBOY CANTER.
    They never lie, sir, between meals. 'Gainst supper
    You may have a bale or two brought in.
FITTON.                              This Canter          40
    Is an old envious knave!
ALMANAC.                    A very rascal!
FITTON.
    I ha' mark'd him all this meal. He has done nothing
    But mock with scurvy faces all we said.
ALMANAC.
    A supercilious rogue! He looks as if
    He were the patrico—
MADRIGAL.                Or archpriest o'canters—          45
SHUNFIELD.
    He's some primate metropolitan rascal,
    Our shot-clog makes so much of him.
ALMANAC.                        The Law
    And he does govern him.
PENNYBOY JUNIOR.          What say you, gentlemen?

---

31–32. *have . . . file*] take precedence.
39. *'Gainst*] against, in preparation for.
45. *patrico*] hedge-priest or parson of the gypsies or beggars.
47. *shot-clog*] a gull who is tolerated because he pays the shot or
reckoning.

FITTON.

    We say we wonder not your man o' law
    Should be so gracious wi' you, but how it comes    50
    This rogue, this Canter—
PENNYBOY JUNIOR.            Oh, good words!
FITTON.                      A fellow
    That speaks no language—
ALMANAC.           But what jingling gypsies,
    And peddlers trade in—
FITTON.            And no honest Christian
    Can understand—
PENNYBOY CANTER.    Why by that argument,
                     *He speaks to all the Jeerers.*
    You all are canters. You and you and you,    55
    All the whole world are canters, I will prove it,
    In your professions.
PENNYBOY JUNIOR.    I would fain hear this.
    But stay, my princess comes. Provide the while,
    I'll call for't anon.

[*Enter* Lickfinger, Pecunia, Statute, Band, Wax, *and* Mortgage.]

                How fares your grace?

[IV.ii]
LICKFINGER.

    I hope the fare was good.
PECUNIA.            Yes, Lickfinger,
    And we shall thank you for't and reward you.

Pennyboy [Junior] *is courting his* Princess *all the while.*

MADRIGAL.

    Nay, I'll not lose my argument, Lickfinger.

[IV.ii]
1.] *preceded in F and F3 by S.D.:*
Lickfinger, Pecunia, Statute, Band,
Wax {to them.
2–5.] *F margin:* "Lickfinger *is*
*challeng'd by* Madrigal *of an ar-*
*gument"; Lickfinger . . . an Argu-*
*ment." F3.*
2.1.] *F prints in margin to left of*
*ll. 42–45.*

[IV.i]
    50. *gracious wi' you*] enjoy your grace.

Before these gentlewomen, I affirm
The perfect and true strain of poetry                          5
Is rather to be given the quick cellar
Than the fat kitchen.
LICKFINGER.                        Heretic, I see
Thou art for the vain oracle of the bottle.
The hogshead, Trismegistus, is thy Pegasus.
Thence flows thy Muse's spring, from that hard hoof.     10
Seduced poet, I do say to thee,
A boiler, range, and dresser were the fountains
Of all the knowledge in the universe.
And they are the kitchens, where the master cook—
(Thou dost not know the man, nor canst thou know him,   15
Till thou hast serv'd some years in that deep school
That's both the nurse and mother of the arts,
And hear'st him read, interpret, and demonstrate!)
A master cook! Why, he's the man o' men
For a professor. He designs, he draws,                          20
He paints, he carves, he builds, he fortifies,
Makes citadels of curious fowl and fish,
Some he dry-ditches, some moats round with broths.
Mounts marrowbones, cuts fifty-angled custards,
Rears bulwark pies, and for his outer-works                    25
He raiseth ramparts of immortal crust,
And teacheth all the tactics at one dinner:
What ranks, what files, to put his dishes in,
The whole art military. Then he knows

---

4. gentlewomen] *Gifford;* gentle-     23. dry-ditches] *H.S.;* dry-dishes,
men *F, F3.*                              *F, F3.*

---

5–40. *The . . . divine*] Except for some minor changes in the first
few lines and the change from "bare-breeched" to "airy" in l. 34,
this passage comes verbatim from *Neptune's Triumph,* ll. 70–112.

8–9. *oracle . . . Trismegistus*] After the oracle of the bottle has
spoken the one word "Trinch" (drink), Panurge uses the phrase "La
Bouteille trymegiste" (the thrice-greatest bottle), Rabelais, *Gargantua
and Pantagruel,* bk. 5, chap. 45.

9–10. *Pegasus . . . hoof*] The springs of Helicon rose from the place
Pegasus' hoof struck on Mount Helicon.

12. *dresser*] table or sideboard on which food was prepared for
cooking.

The influence of the stars upon his meats,                    30
And all their seasons, tempers, qualities,
And so to fit his relishes and sauces,
He has Nature in a pot 'bove all the chemists
Or airy brethren of the Rosy Cross.
He is an architect, an engineer,                    35
A soldier, a physician, a philosopher,
A general mathematician.

MADRIGAL.                    It is granted.

LICKFINGER.

And that you may not doubt him for a poet—

ALMANAC.

This fury shows, if there were nothing else,
And 'tis divine. I shall forever, hereafter,                    40
Admire the wisdom of a cook.

BAND.                    And we, sir!

PENNYBOY JUNIOR.

Oh, how my princess draws me with her looks
And hails me in, as eddies draw in boats
Or strong Charybdis ships that sail too near
The shelves of love! The tides of your two eyes,                    45
Wind of your breath, are such as suck in all
That do approach you.

PECUNIA.                    Who hath chang'd my servant?

PENNYBOY JUNIOR.

Yourself, who drink my blood up with your beams
As doth the sun, the sea. Pecunia shines
More in the world than he, and makes it spring                    50
Where'er she favors. Please her but to show
Her melting wrists or bare her ivory hands,
She catches still! Her smiles they are love's fetters!
Her breasts his apples! Her teats strawberries!
Where Cupid (were he present now) would cry:                    55
Farewell, my mother's milk, here's sweeter nectar!

35. engineer] *F3;* Inginer *F.*          54. strawberries] *F3;* Stawberries
                                                  *F.*

---

34. *Rosy Cross*] See III.ii.99, note.
53. *catches*] captivates.

Help me to praise Pecunia, gentlemen.
She's your princess. Lend your wits.

FITTON.                                    A lady

The Graces taught to move!

ALMANAC.                          The Hours did nurse!

FITTON.

Whose lips are the instructions of all lovers!          60

ALMANAC.

Her eyes their lights and rivals to the stars!

FITTON.

A voice as if that Harmony still spake!

ALMANAC.

And polish'd skin, whiter than Venus' foot—

FITTON.

Young Hebe's neck or Juno's arms!

ALMANAC.                                An air

Large as the morning's and her breath as sweet          65
As meadows after rain and but new-mown!

FITTON.

Leda might yield unto her for a face—

ALMANAC.

Hermione for breasts!

FITTON.                          Flora for cheeks!

ALMANAC.

And Helen for a mouth!

PENNYBOY JUNIOR.                    Kiss, kiss 'em, princess.

                                   *She kisseth them.*

FITTON.

The pearl doth strive in whiteness with her neck—          70

ALMANAC.

But loseth by it. Here the snow thaws snow;
One frost resolves another!

---

59–61.] *F margin: "They all be-*     64. An air] *H.S. conj.;* A haire *F,*
*ginne the encomium of* Pecunia."     *F3.*

---

64. *Juno's arms*] In Iliad 1.595, she is called "white-armed Hera."
68. *Hermione for breasts*] The only offspring of Helen and Menelaus,
her figure was like that of the "golden Aphrodite" (*Odyssey* 4.13–14).
72. *resolves*] dissolves.

FITTON.                              Oh, she has
A front too slippery to be look'd upon—
ALMANAC.
And glances that beguile the seer's eyes!
PENNYBOY JUNIOR.
Kiss, kiss again. What says my man o' war?          75
                              [*She kisseth them*] *again.*
SHUNFIELD.
I say she's more than fame can promise of her,
A theme that's overcome with her own matter!
Praise is struck blind and deaf and dumb with her!
She doth astonish commendation!
PENNYBOY JUNIOR.
Well pump'd i'faith, old sailor. Kiss him, too,      80
Though he be a slug.       *She kisseth* Captain Shunfield.
            What says my poet-sucker?
He's chewing his Muse's cud, I do see by him.
MADRIGAL.
I have almost done. I want but e'en to finish.
FITTON.
That's the ill luck of all his works still.
PENNYBOY JUNIOR.                              What?
FITTON.
To begin many works but finish none.               85
PENNYBOY JUNIOR.
How does he do his mistress' work?
FITTON.                              Imperfect.
ALMANAC.
I cannot think he finisheth that.
PENNYBOY JUNIOR.                    Let's hear.
MADRIGAL.
It is a madrigal. I affect that kind
Of poem much.
PENNYBOY JUNIOR.   And thence you ha' the name.

---

73. *slippery*] dangerous (L. *lubricus*, Horace, *Odes* 1. 29. 8).
81. *slug*] sluggard.
81. *poet-sucker*] sucking or immature poet.

FITTON.

It is his rose. He can make nothing else.            90

MADRIGAL.

I made it to the tune the fiddlers play'd
That we all lik'd so well.

PENNYBOY JUNIOR.                 Good. Read it, read it.

MADRIGAL.

The Sun is father of all metals, you know,
Silver and gold.

PENNYBOY JUNIOR.    Ay, leave your prologues. Say!

MADRIGAL.

*As bright as is the Sun her sire,*                   95
*Or Earth, her mother, in her best attire,*
*Or Mint, the midwife, with her fire,*
*Comes forth her grace!*

PENNYBOY JUNIOR.

That Mint the midwife does well.

MADRIGAL.

*The splendor of the wealthiest mines,*              100
*The stamp and strength of all imperial lines,*
*Both majesty and beauty shines*

FITTON.

That's fairly said of money.

MADRIGAL.

*In her sweet face!*
*Look how a torch, of taper light,*                  105
*Or of that torch's flame, a beacon bright—*

PENNYBOY JUNIOR.

Good!

95.] *preceded in F and F3 by*
SONG.
99–111.] *F prints l. 99 next to ll.*
*98 and 100, l. 103 next to ll. 102*
*and 104, l. 107 next to l. 106, and*
*l. 111 next to l. 110, to indicate*
*that they are spoken during the*
*song.*

---

90. *his rose*] Jonson tells the anecdote of "a painter who can paint
nothing but a Rose," a practice he justified by arguing that "a Rose
is above" all else, in *Conversations with Drummond,* ll. 490–92.

105. *light*] past participle still in use despite the newer form *lit*
(Partridge, p. 184).

MADRIGAL.

Now there, I want a line to finish, sir.

PENNYBOY JUNIOR.

*Or of that beacon's fire, moonlight.*

MADRIGAL.

*So takes she place!*                                                    110

FITTON.

'Tis good.

MADRIGAL.

And then I have a saraband—
*She makes good cheer, she keeps full boards,*
*She holds a fair of knights and lords,*
*A market of all offices*                                                115
*And shops of honor more or less.*
*According to Pecunia's grace,*
*The bride hath beauty, blood, and place,*
*The bridegroom virtue, valor, wit,*
*And wisdom, as he stands for it.*                                       120

PENNYBOY JUNIOR.

Call in the fiddlers.

[*Enter the* Fiddlers *and* Nicholas.]

Nick, the boy, shall sing it.
Sweet princess, kiss him. Kiss 'em all, dear madam,
And at the close, vouchsafe to call them cousins.

PECUNIA.

Sweet cousin Madrigal and cousin Fitton,
My cousin Shunfield and my learned cousin—                               125

[*As she kisses them.*]

PICKLOCK.

Al-manach, though they call him Almanac.

PENNYBOY CANTER [*aside*].

Why, here's the prodigal prostitutes his mistress!

---

121–23.] *F margin: "He vrgeth her*      121. S.P.] *1716;* Pic. *F, F3.*
*to kisse them all."*                     126. S.P.] *Gifford;* P. Ca. *F, F3.*
                                          127. S.P.] *Gifford;* P. Iv. *F, F3.*

---

110. *place*] precedence.

PENNYBOY JUNIOR.

    And Picklock, he must be a kinsman, too.

    My man o' law will teach us all to win,

    And keep our own. Old Founder—

PENNYBOY CANTER.             Nothing, I, sir.    130

    I am a wretch, a beggar. She the fortunate

    Can want no kindred, we the poor know none.

FITTON.

    Nor none shall know by my consent.

ALMANAC.                Nor mine.

PENNYBOY JUNIOR.

    Sing, boy, stand here.

*The* Boy *sings the song.*

PENNYBOY CANTER [*aside*]. Look, look, how all their eyes

    Dance i' their heads (observe) scatter'd with lust    135

    At sight o' their brave idol! How they are tickl'd

    With a light air, the bawdy saraband!

    They are a kind of dancing engines all,

    And set by nature, thus to run alone

    To every sound! All things within, without them,    140

    Move, but their brain, and that stands still! Mere monsters,

    Here in a chamber, of most subtle feet!

    And make their legs in tune, passing the streets!

    These are the gallant spirits o'the age,

    The miracles o'the time, that can cry up    145

    And down men's wits and set what rate on things

    Their half-brain'd fancies please! Now pox upon 'em!

    See how solicitously he learns the jig

    As if it were a mystery of his faith!

SHUNFIELD.

    A dainty ditty!

FITTON.          Oh, he's a dainty poet    150

    When he sets to't.

---

140. without] *F3;* withou *F.*

---

145–46. *cry . . . down*] extol and decry.

149. *mystery*] rite.

PENNYBOY JUNIOR.          And a dainty scholar!

ALMANAC.

No, no great scholar, he writes like a gentleman.

SHUNFIELD.

Pox o' your scholar!

PENNYBOY CANTER [*aside*].   Pox o' your distinction!
As if a scholar were no gentleman.
With these, to write like a gentleman will in time          155
Become all one as to write like an ass.
These gentlemen? These rascals! I am sick
Of indignation at 'em.

PENNYBOY JUNIOR.          How do you like't, sir?

FITTON.

'Tis excellent.

ALMANAC.          'Twas excellently sung.

FITTON.

A dainty air.

PENNYBOY JUNIOR.   What says my Lickfinger?          160

LICKFINGER.

I am telling Mistress Band and Mistress Statute
What a brave gentleman you are, and Wax here!
How much 'twere better that my lady's grace
Would here take up, sir, and keep house with you.

PENNYBOY JUNIOR.

What say they?

STATUTE.          We could consent, sir, willingly.          165

BAND.

Ay, if we knew her grace had the least liking.

WAX.

We must obey her grace's will and pleasure.

PENNYBOY JUNIOR.

I thank you, gentlewomen. Ply 'em, Lickfinger.
Give Mother Mortgage, there—

---

151–52.] *F margin: "They are all
struck with admiration."*
157. gentlemen] *F3;* Centlemen *F.*

162. gentleman] *F3;* Centleman *F.*
168. gentlewomen] *F;* Gentlewom-
an *F3.*

LICKFINGER.                         Her dose of sack.

I have it for her, and her distance of hum.                    170

*The* Gallants *are all about* Pecunia.

PECUNIA.

Indeed, therein I must confess, dear cousin,

I am a most unfortunate princess.

ALMANAC.                          And

You still will be so when your grace may help it?

MADRIGAL.

Who'd lie in a room with a close-stool and garlic

And kennel with his dogs that had a prince                    175

Like this young Pennyboy to sojourn with?

SHUNFIELD.

He'll let you ha' your liberty—

ALMANAC.                          Go forth

Whither you please and to what company—

MADRIGAL.

Scatter yourself amongst us—

PENNYBOY JUNIOR.                 Hope of Parnassus!

Thy ivy shall not wither nor thy bays;                        180

Thou shalt be had into her grace's cellar

And there know sack and claret all December.

Thy vein is rich, and we must cherish it.

Poets and bees swarm nowadays, but yet

There are not those good taverns for the one sort            185

As there are flow'ry fields to feed the other.

Though bees be pleas'd with dew, ask little Wax

That brings the honey to her lady's hive,

The poet must have wine. And he shall have it.


[IV.iii]                [*Enter*] Pennyboy Senior

PENNYBOY SENIOR.

Broker, what, Broker!

0.1.] Pennyboy Senior, Pennyboy
Junior, Lickfinger, &c. *F, F3.*

---

170. *distance*] quantity measured by the mark or peg in a drinking
vessel.

170. *hum*] strong ale.

174. *close-stool*] chamber pot enclosed in a stool or box.

PENNYBOY JUNIOR.          Who's that?  My uncle!
PENNYBOY SENIOR.
    I am abus'd.  Where is my knave, my broker?
LICKFINGER.
    Your broker is laid out upon a bench yonder.
    Sack hath seiz'd on him in the shape of sleep.
PICKLOCK.
    He hath been dead to us almost this hour.                    5
PENNYBOY SENIOR.
    This hour?
PENNYBOY CANTER.   Why sigh you, sir? 'Cause he's at rest?
PENNYBOY SENIOR.
    It breeds my unrest.
LICKFINGER.               Will you take a cup
    And try if you can sleep?
PENNYBOY SENIOR.                   No, cogging Jack,
    Thou and thy cups, too, perish!

          *He strikes the sack out of his hand.*

SHUNFIELD.                        Oh, the sack!
MADRIGAL.
    The sack, the sack!
PENNYBOY CANTER.     A madrigal on sack!                    10
PICKLOCK.
    Or rather an elegy, for the sack is gone.
PECUNIA.
    Why do you this, sir?  Spill the wine and rave
    For Broker's sleeping?
PENNYBOY SENIOR.          What through sleep and sack
    My trust is wrong'd, but I am still awake
    To wait upon your grace.  Please you to quit                    15
    This strange, lewd company.  They are not for you.
PECUNIA.
    No, guardian, I do like them very well.
PENNYBOY SENIOR.
    Your grace's pleasure be observ'd, but you,
    Statute and Band and Wax, will go with me.

---

13. Broker's] *F;* Booker's *F3.*      *haue* Pecunia *home. But shee re-*
15–20.] *F margin: "Hee would*     *fuseth. And her Traine."*

STATUTE.

    Truly we will not.

BAND.                    We will stay and wait here                    20

    Upon her grace and this your noble kinsman.

PENNYBOY SENIOR.

    Noble? How noble? Who hath made him noble?

PENNYBOY JUNIOR.

    Why, my most noble money hath, or shall,

    My princess here. She that had you but kept

    And treated kindly would have made you noble,              25

    And wise too. Nay, perhaps have done that for you

    An Act of Parliament could not, made you honest.

    The truth is, uncle, that her grace dislikes

    Her entertainment, specially her lodging.

PECUNIA.

    Nay, say her jail. Never unfortunate princess              30

    Was us'd so by a jailer. Ask my women.

    Band, you can tell, and Statute, how he has us'd me,

    Kept me close prisoner, under twenty bolts—

STATUTE.

    And forty padlocks—

BAND.                    All malicious engines

    A wicked smith could forge out of his iron—                35

    As locks, and keys, shackles, and manacles—

    To torture a great lady.

STATUTE.                    H'has abus'd

    Your grace's body.

PECUNIA.                    No, he would ha' done;

    That lay not in his power. He had the use

    Of your bodies, Band and Wax, and sometimes Statute's.    40

    But once he would ha' smother'd me in a chest

    And strangl'd me in leather, but that you

    Came to my rescue then and gave me air.

40. your] *S. T. Coleridge, cited by*
*de Winter; our F, F3.*

---

23. *my . . . money hath*] an allusion to King James I's practice of
creating peerages and selling them to the highest bidder.

STATUTE.

> For which he cramm'd us up in a close box,
> All three together, where we saw no sun          45
> In one six-months.

WAX.                 A cruel man he is!

BAND.

> H'has left my fellow Wax out, i'the cold—

STATUTE.

> Till she was stiff as any frost, and crumbl'd
> Away to dust and almost lost her form.

WAX.

> Much ado to reçover me.

PENNYBOY SENIOR.         Women jeerers!      50

> Have you learn'd too the subtle faculty?
> Come, I'll show you the way home if drink
> Or too full diet have disguis'd you.

BAND.                 Troth,

> We have not any mind, sir, of return—

STATUTE.

> To be bound back to back—

BAND.            And have our legs      55

> Turn'd in or writh'd about—

WAX.            Or else display'd—

STATUTE.

> Be lodg'd with dust and fleas as we were wont—

BAND.

> And dieted with dogs' dung.

PENNYBOY SENIOR.         Why, you whores,

> My bawds, my instruments! What should I call you,
> Man may think base enough for you?

PENNYBOY JUNIOR.         Hear you, uncle.   60

> I must not hear this of my princess' servants,
> And in Apollo, in Pecunia's room.
> Go, get you down the stairs. Home, to your kennel,

---

53. *disguis'd you*] made you drunk.

59. *instruments*] with a triple pun on "instrument" meaning (1) tool, (2) document, and (3) the female sex organ.

62. *Apollo . . . room*] In alchemy, Apollo or the sun signifies gold; see also II.v.127, note.

As swiftly as you can. Consult your dogs,
The *lares* of your family, or believe it,                    65
The fury of a footman and a drawer
Hangs over you.
SHUNFIELD.                    Cudgel and pot do threaten
A kind of vengeance.
MADRIGAL.                    Barbers are at hand.
                                        *They all threaten.*

ALMANAC.
Washing and shaving will ensue.
FITTON.                              The pump
Is not far off. If 'twere, the sink is near                    70
Or a good jordan.
MADRIGAL.                    You have now no money—
SHUNFIELD.
But are a rascal.
PENNYBOY SENIOR.    I am cheated, robb'd,
Jeer'd by confederacy.
FITTON.                              No, you are kick'd
And used kindly, as you should be.

    *And [they] spurn him [and start to] kick him out.*

SHUNFIELD.                              Spurn'd
From all commerce of men, who are a cur.                    75
ALMANAC.
A stinking dog in a doublet, with foul linen—
MADRIGAL.
A snarling rascal. Hence!
SHUNFIELD.                    Out!
PENNYBOY SENIOR.                    Well, remember
I am cozen'd by my cousin and his whore.
Bane o'these meetings in Apollo!


77–78.] F *margin: "Hee exclaimes."*

---

66. *drawer*] tapster.
71. *jordan*] chamber pot.

LICKFINGER.                                    Go, sir,
You will be toss'd like Block in a blanket else.                    80
PENNYBOY JUNIOR.
Down with him, Lickfinger.
PENNYBOY SENIOR.                    Saucy Jack, away.
Pecunia is a whore.
PENNYBOY JUNIOR.          Play him down, fiddlers,
And drown his noise.

[*Enter* Piedmantle *and exeunt* Pennyboy Senior *and* Lickfinger.]

                              Who's this?
FITTON.                              Oh, Master Piedmantle!


[IV.iv]

          Piedmantle *brings the* Lady Pecunia *her pedigree.*

PIEDMANTLE.
By your leave, gentlemen.
FITTON.                              Her grace's herald.
ALMANAC.
No herald yet, a heraldet.
PENNYBOY JUNIOR.              What's that?
PENNYBOY CANTER.
A canter.
PENNYBOY JUNIOR.    Oh, thou said'st thou'dst prove us all so!
PENNYBOY CANTER.
Sir, here is one will prove himself so, straight.
So shall the rest in time.
PECUNIA.                         My pedigree?                    5
I tell you, friend, he must be a good scholar,

---

[IV.iii]
80. Block] *identified in the mar-*
*gin of F as "One of his Dogges."*

[IV.iv]
0.1.] Piedmantle (*to them. F, F3.*
*F prints S.D. in margin beside ll.*
*1–4.*
3. prove] *F3;* sproue *F.*

---

[IV.iii]
   80. *Block*] Although Block is identified as one of Pennyboy Senior's
dogs in the marginal note, it is not clear what this allusion meant to
the audience here; see also V.iii.42–43.

Can my descent. I am of princely race,
And as good blood as any is i'the mines
Runs through my veins. I am every limb a princess!
Duchess o'Mines was my great grandmother,                10
And by the father's side I come from Sol.
My grandfather was Duke of Or and match'd
In the blood royal of Ophir.

PIEDMANTLE.                    Here's his coat.

PECUNIA.

I know it if I hear the blazon.

PIEDMANTLE.                    He bears
In a field azure, a sun proper, beamy,                    15
Twelve of the second.

PENNYBOY CANTER.        How far's this from canting?

PENNYBOY JUNIOR.

Her grace doth understand it.

PENNYBOY CANTER.                She can cant, sir.

PECUNIA.

What be these? Besants?

PIEDMANTLE.                    Yes, an't please your grace.

PECUNIA.

That is our coat, too, as we come from Or.
What line's this?

PIEDMANTLE.            The rich mines of Potosi,          20

17. it] *F3;* ti *F.*

---

7. *Can*] knows.

11–12. *Sol . . . Or*] Both *Sol* and *or* are used for gold in describing coats of arms; descriptions by names and planets (e.g., Sol, Luna, Mars) were usually reserved for kings and princes whereas the usual method was by the names of metals and colors (e.g., or, argent, azure).

13. *coat*] coat of arms.

14. *blazon*] description of armorial bearings according to the rules of heraldry.

15. *azure*] blue (heraldic).

15. *proper*] heraldic term meaning having its natural color; it would therefore be or (gold).

15. *beamy*] having beams or rays (heraldic).

16. *of the second*] of the second tincture named, that is, or.

18. *Besants*] small gold circles (heraldic).

20. *Potosi*] Mount Potosi in Bolivia, where silver was discovered in the sixteenth century.

The Spanish mines i'the West Indies.

PECUNIA.                                    This?

PIEDMANTLE.

The mines o' Hungary, this of Barbary.

PECUNIA.

But this, this little branch?

PIEDMANTLE.                        The Welsh mine that.

PECUNIA.

I ha' Welsh blood in me, too. Blaze, sir, that coat.

PIEDMANTLE.

She bears (an't please you) argent, three leeks vert          25
In canton or, and tassel'd of the first.

PENNYBOY CANTER.

Is not this canting? Do you understand him?

PENNYBOY JUNIOR.

Not I. But it sounds well, and the whole thing
Is rarely painted. I will have such a scroll
Whate'er it cost me.

PECUNIA.                    Well, at better leisure          30
We'll take a view of it and so reward you.

PENNYBOY JUNIOR.

Kiss him, sweet princess, and style him a cousin.

PECUNIA.

I will, if you will have it. Cousin Piedmantle.

*She kisseth* [Piedmantle].

PENNYBOY JUNIOR.

I love all men of virtue, from my princess

23. S.P. PIEDMANTLE.] *1716;* Pec. *F,*
*F3.*

---

24. *Blaze*] to blazon.
25. *bears*] is entitled to display heraldically.
25. *argent*] silver (heraldic).
25. *leeks*] emblem of Wales, conspicuously absent from heraldic works.
25. *vert*] green (heraldic).
26. *canton*] a square division less than a quarter, occupying the upper (usually dexter) corner of a shield.
26. *tassel'd of the first*] having tassels of the tincture first mentioned in the blazon, that is, argent.

Unto my beggar here, old Canter. On,                    35
On to thy proof. Whom prove you the next canter?

PENNYBOY CANTER.

The doctor here. I will proceed with the learned.
When he discourseth of *dissection*
Or any point of *anatomy*, that he tells you
Of *vena cava* and of *vena porta*,                    40
The *meseraicks* and the *mesenterium*,
What does he else but cant? Or if he run
To his *judicial astrology*
And trowl the *trine*, the *quartile*, and the *sextile*,
*Platic aspect*, and *partile*, with his *hyleg*                    45
Or *alchochoden, cuspes,* and *horoscope,*
Does not he cant? Who here does understand him?

ALMANAC.

This is no canter, though.

PENNYBOY CANTER.                    Or when my muster-master
Talks of his *tactics* and his *ranks* and *files,*
His *bringers up,* his *leaders on,* and cries,                    50

---

40. *vena cava*] one of the main veins opening into the right atrium
of the heart.

40. *vena porta*] the large vein formed by the union of veins from
the stomach, intestines, and spleen, conveying blood to the liver.

41. *meseraicks . . . mesenterium*] Both are names for the mesentery,
the double layer of peritoneal membrane which supports the small
intestine.

43. *judicial astrology*] astrology in the modern sense as distinguished
from natural astrology, which predicted natural phenomena such as
tides.

44. *trowl*] sing as a catch.

44. *trine . . . sextile*] Planets 120 degrees, 90 degrees, and 60 degrees
distant from one another are said to be in trine, quartile, and sextile
aspects, respectively.

45. *Platic*] pertaining to or in the position of a ray cast from one
planet to another, not exactly, but within the orbit of its own light.

45. *partile*] exact to the same degree and minute, or at least to
within a degree.

45. *hyleg*] ruling planet of a nativity.

46. *alcochoden*] planet which indicates by its position the length
of life.

46. *cuspes*] The cusp is the opening or entrance of an astrological
house.

50. *bringers up*] last rank.

    *Faces about to the right hand, the left,*
    Now, *as you were,* then tells you of *redoubts,*
    Of *cats* and *cortines,* doth not he cant?

PENNYBOY JUNIOR.             Yes, faith.

PENNYBOY CANTER.

    My egg-chinn'd laureat, here, when he comes forth
    With *dimeters* and *trimeters, tetrameters,*       55
    *Pentameters, hexameters, catalectics,*
    His *hyper-* and his *brachy-catalectics,*
    His *pyrrhics, epitrites,* and *choriambics,*
    What is all this but canting?

MADRIGAL.             A rare fellow!

SHUNFIELD.

    Some begging scholar.

FITTON.           A decay'd doctor at least!     60

PENNYBOY JUNIOR.

    Nay, I do cherish virtue though in rags.

PENNYBOY CANTER.

    And you, Mas Courtier.

PENNYBOY JUNIOR.       Now he treats of you.
    Stand forth to him fair.

PENNYBOY CANTER.       With all your fly-blown projects
    And looks-out of the politics, your shut-faces
    And reserv'd questions, and answers that you
        game with, as—            65
    Is't a *clear business?* Will it *manage well?*
    *My name* must not be us'd else. Here 'twill *dash.*

---

    53. *cats*] movable penthouses used by besiegers to protect themselves while approaching fortifications.

    53. *cortines*] plain wall of a fortified place, the part of the wall that connects two bastions or towers, for example.

    56. *catalectics*] verses lacking a syllable in the last foot.

    57. *hyper-* . . . *brachy-catalectics*] verses having one or two syllables after the last foot and verses lacking two syllables in the last foot, respectively.

    58. *pyrrhics*] metrical feet made up of two short syllables.

    58. *epitrites*] metrical feet made up of three long and one short syllable in any order.

    58. *choriambics*] four-syllable feet: long, short, short, long.

    67. *dash*] destroy, ruin.

Your *business has receiv'd a taint;* give off,
I may not *prostitute myself.* Tut, tut,
*That little dust I can blow off* at pleasure.                    70
*Here's no such mountain yet i'the whole work*
*But a light purse may level.* I will *tide*
*This affair* for you, give it *freight* and *passage—*
And such mint-phrase, as 'tis the worst of canting
By how much it affects the sense it has not.                    75

FITTON.

This is some other than he seems.

PENNYBOY JUNIOR.                    How like you him?

FITTON.

This cannot be a canter.

PENNYBOY JUNIOR.                    But he is, sir,
And shall be still and so shall you be too.
We'll all be canters. Now I think of it,
A noble whimsy's come into my brain.                    80
I'll build a college, I and my Pecunia,
And call it Canters' College. Sounds it well?

ALMANAC.

Excellent!

PENNYBOY JUNIOR.    And here stands my Father Rector.
And you professors, you shall all profess
Something and live there with her grace and me,                    85
Your founders. I'll endow't with lands and means,
And Lickfinger shall be my master-cook.
What, is he gone?

PENNYBOY CANTER.    And a professor.

PENNYBOY JUNIOR.                    Yes.

PENNYBOY CANTER.

And read Apicius *de re culinaria*
To your brave doxy and you.

81–83.] *F    margin:* "Canters-Col-
ledge, *begun to be erected.*"

68. *give off*] leave off.
89. *Apicius . . . culinaria*] a third-century collection of recipes
falsely attributed to the Roman gourmand H. Gabius Apicius, who
lived in the reign of Tiberius.
90. *doxy*] the mistress of a beggar (slang).

PENNYBOY JUNIOR.                    You, cousin Fitton,          90
   Shall (as a courtier) read the politics.
   Doctor Almanac, he shall read astrology.
   Shunfield shall read the military arts.
PENNYBOY CANTER.
   As carving, and assaulting the cold custard.
PENNYBOY JUNIOR.
   And Horace here, the art of poetry,                          95
   His lyrics and his madrigals, fine songs,
   Which we will have at dinner, steep'd in claret,
   And against supper, sous'd in sack.
MADRIGAL.                                In troth
   A divine whimsy!
SHUNFIELD.                      And a worthy work,
   Fit for a chronicle.
PENNYBOY JUNIOR.          Is't not?
SHUNFIELD.                               To all ages.          100
PENNYBOY JUNIOR.
   And Piedmantle shall give us all our arms.
   But Picklock, what wouldst thou be? Thou canst cant too.
PICKLOCK.
   In all the languages in Westminster Hall,
   Pleas, Bench, or Chancery; *fee-farm, fee-tail,*
   *Tenant in dower, at will, for term of life,*              105
   By *copy of court roll, knights' service, homage,*

94–95.] *F margin: "That's* Madri-
gall."

---

   98. *against*] in preparation for.
   104. *fee-farm*] land held in perpetuity subject to a fixed rent with
no other services.
   104. *fee-tail*] an inheritable estate which can descend to certain
classes of heirs only.
   105. *Tenant in dower*] a widow who holds for life a part of her
dead husband's estate.
   105. *at will*] an estate held during the owner's pleasure.
   106. *court roll*] the records in a manor, in which names, rents, and
services of the tenants, or copyholders, were enrolled.

*Fealty, escuage, soccage* or *frank almoigne,*
*Grand sergeanty,* or *burgage.*

PENNYBOY JUNIOR.                    Thou appear'st,
Κατ ἐξοχὴν a canter. Thou shalt read
All Littleton's *Tenures* to me and indeed          110
All my conveyances.

PICKLOCK.                    And make 'em too, sir!
Keep all your courts, be steward o' your lands,
Let all your leases, keep your evidences.
But first, I must procure and pass your mortmain.
You must have license from above, sir.

PENNYBOY JUNIOR.                    Fear not.          115
Pecunia's friends shall do it.

*Here his father [throws off his patched cloak and] discovers*
*himself.*

PENNYBOY CANTER.                    But I shall stop it!
Your worship's loving and obedient father,
Your painful steward, and lost officer,
Who have done this to try how you would use
Pecunia when you had her, which since I see,          120

---

107. *Fealty*] the fidelity of a feudal tenant to his lord.
107. *escuage*] literally, shield-service, the chief form of feudal tenure.
107. *soccage*] tenure of lands by performing certain agricultural services.
107. *frank almoigne*] tenure whereby a religious corporation holds lands in consideration of religious services it performs.
108. *Grand sergeanty*] species of service which cannot be due to any lord from a tenant but must consist in some service immediately respecting the person or dignity of the sovereign, e.g., to be his marshal or carry his standard.
108. *burgage*] tenure in boroughs whereby lands or tenements were held of the king or other lord of the borough at a certain yearly rent.
109. Κατ' ἐξοχὴν] par excellence.
110. *Littleton's Tenures*] the great fifteenth-century treatise on land law, which had gone through sixty editions by the time of the play. Sir Edward Coke, whose name provides a pun at V.vi.46, had written a famous commentary on Littleton.
114–15. *mortmain . . . license*] Since property in mortmain is held inalienably by a corporation, the king's permission had to be sought to alienate such property.
118. *painful*] painstaking.

I will take home the lady to my charge,
And these her servants, and leave you my cloak
To travel in to Beggars' Bush. A seat
Is built already, furnish'd too, worth twenty
Of your imagin'd structures, Canters' College.          125

FITTON.

'Tis his father!

MADRIGAL.                   He's alive methinks.

ALMANAC.

I knew he was no rogue.

PENNYBOY CANTER.                   Thou prodigal,
Was I so careful for thee, to procure
And plot wi' my learn'd counsel, Master Picklock,
This noble match for thee? And dost thou prostitute,  130
Scatter thy mistress' favors, throw away
Her bounties, as they were red-burning coals
Too hot for thee to handle, on such rascals,
Who are the scum and excrements of men?
If thou hadst sought out good and virtuous persons    135
Of these professions, I had lov'd thee and them.
For these shall never have that plea 'gainst me,
Or color of advantage, that I hate
Their callings, but their manners and their vices.
A worthy courtier is the ornament                     140
Of a king's palace, his great master's honor.
[*Points to* Fitton.]  This is a moth, a rascal, a court rat
That gnaws the commonwealth with broking suits
And eating grievances!  So, a true soldier,
He is his country's strength, his sovereign's safety,  145
And to secure his peace, he makes himself
The heir of danger, nay the subject of it,
And runs those virtuous hazards that this scarecrow
Cannot endure to hear of.

SHUNFIELD.                   You are pleasant, sir.

142. S.D.] *Gifford.*

---

123. *Beggars' Bush*] Ray says it is a "tree notoriously known, on the
left hand of the London Road from Huntington to Caxton."
128. *careful*] full of care, anxious.

PENNYBOY CANTER.

With you I dare be. Here is Piedmantle.     150
'Cause he's an ass, do not I love a herald
Who is the pure preserver of descents,
The keeper fair of all nobility,
Without which all would run into confusion?
Were he a learned herald, I would tell him     155
He can give arms and marks, he cannot honor,
No more than money can make noble. It may
Give place and rank, but it can give no virtue.
And he would thank me for this truth. This dog-leech,
You style him Doctor, 'cause he can compile     160
An almanac, perhaps erect a scheme
For my great madam's monkey when't has ta'en
A glister, and beray'd the ephemerides.
Do I despise a learn'd physician,
In calling him a quacksalver? Or blast     165
The ever-living garland, always green,
Of a good poet, when I say his wreath
Is piec'd and patch'd of dirty wither'd flowers?
Away, I am impatient of these ulcers
(That I not call you worse). There is no sore     170
Or plague but you to infect the times. I abhor
Your very scent. Come, lady, since my prodigal
Knew not to entertain you to your worth,
I'll see if I have learn'd how to receive you
With more respect to you and your fair train here.     175
Farewell, my beggar in velvet, for today.

*He points him to his patch'd cloak thrown off.*

Tomorrow you may put on that grave robe
And enter your great work of Canters' College,
Your work and worthy of a Chronicle.     [*Exeunt.*]

---

151–54. *do not . . . confusion*] traditionally interpreted as homage to Jonson's great teacher William Camden (d. 1623) at Westminster School, who had been Clarenceux king-of-arms, one of the three chief officers of the College of Heralds, for over twenty years.
161. *scheme*] horoscope.
163. *glister*] clyster, enema.
163. *beray'd*] fouled with ordure.

## THE FOURTH INTERMEAN AFTER THE FOURTH ACT

TATTLE.

Why, this was the worst of all, the catastrophe!

CENSURE.

The matter began to be good but now, and he has spoil'd
it all with his beggar there.

MIRTH.

A beggarly Jack it is, I warrant him, and a kin to the
poet.                                                                                                        5

TATTLE.

Like enough, for he had the chiefest part in his play,
if you mark it.

EXPECTATION.

Absurdity on him, for a huge overgrown playmaker!
Why should he make him live again when they and we
all thought him dead? If he had left him to his rags,    10
there had been an end of him.

TATTLE.

Ay, but set a beggar on horseback, he'll never lin till
he be a-gallop.

CENSURE.

The young heir grew a fine gentleman in this last act.

EXPECTATION.

So he did, gossip, and kept the best company.                    15

CENSURE.

And feasted 'em and his mistress.

TATTLE.

And show'd her to 'em all, was not jealous—

MIRTH.

But very communicative and liberal and began to be
magnificent if the churl his father would have let him
alone.                                                                                                       20

CENSURE.

It was spitefully done o'the poet, to make the chuff

---

12–13. *set . . . a-gallop*] proverb: "Set a beggar on horseback and
he will ride a gallop" (Tilley, B 238).

12. *lin*] cease.

21. *chuff*] churl.

take him off in his height, when he was going to do all
his brave deeds!

EXPECTATION.

To found an academy—

TATTLE.

Erect a college—                                            25

EXPECTATION.

Plant his professors, and water his lectures—

MIRTH.

With wine, gossips, as he meant to do, and then to
defraud his purposes—

EXPECTATION.

Kill the hopes of so many towardly young spirits—

TATTLE.

As the doctor's—                                            30

CENSURE.

And the courtier's! I protest, I was in love with Master
Fitton. He did wear all he had, from the hatband to the
shoe-tie, so politically, and would stoop and leer—

MIRTH.

And lie so, in wait for a piece of wit, like a mousetrap!

EXPECTATION.

Indeed, gossip, so would the little doctor. All his        35
behavior was mere glister! O' my conscience, he would
make any party's physic i'the world work with his
discourse.

MIRTH.

I wonder they would suffer it, a foolish old fornicating
father to ravish away his son's mistress—                   40

CENSURE.

And all her women at once, as he did!

TATTLE.

I would ha' flien in his gypsy's face i'faith.

22. height] *F3;* heighth *F.*          42. flien] *F;* flown *F3.*

---

29. *towardly*] promising.
36. *glister*] Expectation puns on the two meanings: (1) luster and
(2) enema.
42. *gypsy's*] The term "gypsy" was loosely applied to rogues and
vagabonds.

MIRTH.

It was a plain piece of political incest and worthy to
be brought afore the high commission of wit. Suppose
we were to censure him. You are the youngest voice,    45
Gossip Tattle, begin.

TATTLE.

Marry, I would ha' the old cony-catcher cozen'd of all
he has, i'the young heir's defense, by his learn'd counsel,
Master Picklock!

CENSURE.

I would rather the courtier had found out some trick to    50
beg him from his estate.

EXPECTATION.

Or the captain had courage enough to beat him.

CENSURE.

Or the fine madrigal-man in rhyme to have run him
out o'the country like an Irish rat.

TATTLE.

No, I would have Master Piedmantle, her grace's herald,    55
to pluck down his hatchments, reverse his coat armor,
and nullify him for no gentleman.

EXPECTATION.

Nay, then let Master Doctor dissect him, have him
open'd, and his tripes translated to Lickfinger to make
a probation dish of.                                        60

48. learn'd] *F;* learned *F3.*         51. from] *F;* for *F3.*

---

44. *high . . . wit*] body of critics; a commission is a body empow-
ered to conduct an investigation.

47. *cony-catcher*] confidence man.

51. *beg . . . estate*] as a reward for informing.

53–54. reflecting the Irish superstition that a bard could get rid
of rats.

55–57. *I . . . gentleman*] parts of the ceremony of degradation.

56. *hatchments*] escutcheons or ensigns armorial granted in honor
of some achievement.

56. *coat armor*] originally arms emblazoned on a surcoat to be worn
over armor; by Jonson's time, arms however displayed.

57. *gentleman*] man entitled to coat arms.

59. *translated*] removed or conveyed.

60. *probation dish*] a test of cookery.

CENSURE. TATTLE.

Agreed! Agreed!

MIRTH.

Faith, I would have him flat disinherited by a decree of court, bound to make restitution of the Lady Pecunia and the use of her body to his son—

EXPECTATION.

And her train, to the gentlemen—                                                65

CENSURE.

And both the poet and himself, to ask them all forgiveness—

TATTLE.

And us, too.

CENSURE.

In two large sheets of paper—

EXPECTATION.

Or to stand in a skin of parchment (which the court   70 please)—

CENSURE.

And those fill'd with news—

MIRTH.

And dedicated to the sustaining of the Staple—

EXPECTATION.

Which their poet hath let fall most abruptly!

MIRTH.

Bankruptly indeed!                                                              75

CENSURE.

You say wittily, gossip, and therefore let a protest go out against him—

MIRTH.

A mournival of protests, or a gleek at least—

EXPECTATION.

In all our names—

CENSURE.

For a decay'd wit—                                                             80

---

70. *skin of parchment*] a sheet of parchment.

78. *mournival*] four aces or face cards, generalized to four of anything.

78. *gleek*] three aces or face cards, generalized to three of anything.

EXPECTATION.

    Broken—

TATTLE.

    Nonsolvent—

CENSURE.

    And forever, forfeit—

MIRTH.

    To scorn, of Mirth—

CENSURE.

    Censure—                             85

EXPECTATION.

    Expectation—

TATTLE.

    Subsign'd Tattle. Stay, they come again.

[V.i]

[*Enter*] Pennyboy Junior; *he comes out in the patch'd cloak his father left him.*

PENNYBOY JUNIOR.

    Nay, they are fit as they had been made for me,
    And I am now a thing worth looking at,
    The same I said I would be in the morning.
    No rogue at a *comitia* of the canters
    Did ever there become his parent's robes         5
    Better than I do these. Great fool and beggar!
    Why do not all that are of those societies
    Come forth and gratulate me one of theirs?
    Methinks I should be on every side saluted
    Dauphin of Beggars, Prince of Prodigals,      10
    That have so fall'n under the ears and eyes
    And tongues of all, the fable o'the time,
    Matter of scorn and mark of reprehension!

0.1–0.2.] Pennyboy Junior {*to him*    1. are] *F; ere F3.*
Thomas Barber {*after,* Picklock.    12. o'] *F; of F3.*
*F, F3. prints* he . . . him *in margin beside ll. 1–4.*

---

4. *comitia*] assembly.
8. *gratulate*] welcome.

I now begin to see my vanity
Shine in this glass, reflected by the foil.                    15
Where is my fashioner, my featherman,
My linener, perfumer, barber, all
That tail of riot follow'd me this morning?
Not one! But a dark solitude about me,
Worthy my cloak and patches, as I had                    20
The epidemical disease upon me.
And I'll sit down with it.                    [*He sits on the floor.*]

[*Enter* Thomas Barber.]

THOMAS BARBER.                    My master! Maker!
How do you? Why do you sit thus o'the ground, sir?
Hear you the news?
PENNYBOY JUNIOR.                    No, nor I care to hear none.
Would I could here sit still and slip away                    25
The other one and twenty to have this
Forgotten and the day ras'd out, expung'd,
In every ephemerides or almanac.
Or if it must be in, that Time and Nature
Have decree'd, still, let it be a day                    30
Of tickling prodigals about the gills,
Deluding gaping heirs, losing their loves
And their discretions, falling from the favors
Of their best friends and parents, their own hopes,
And ent'ring the society of canters.                    35
THOMAS BARBER.
A doleful day it is, and dismal times
Are come upon us. I am clear undone.
PENNYBOY JUNIOR.
How, Tom?
THOMAS BARBER.    Why, broke, broke, wretchedly broke.
PENNYBOY JUNIOR.                    Ha!

27. ras'd] *this edn.;* rac'd *F;* raz'd        32. losing *F3;* loosing *F.*
*F3.*                                                        34. parents] *F;* Parent *F3.*

---

18. *tail of riot*] band of loose-living followers.
21. *epidemical disease*] plague.
27. *ras'd*] erased.

THOMAS BARBER.
    Our Staple is all to pieces, quite dissolv'd.

PENNYBOY JUNIOR.                        Ha!

THOMAS BARBER.
    Shiver'd, as in an earthquake! Heard you not        40
    The crack and ruins? We are all blown up!
    Soon as they heard th'Infanta was got from them,
    Whom they had so devoured i'their hopes,
    To be their patroness and sojourn with 'em,
    Our emissaries, Register, Examiner,               45
    Flew into vapor; our grave governor
    Into a subtler air; and is return'd
    (As we do hear) grand-captain of the jeerers.
    I and my fellow melted into butter
    And spoil'd our ink, and so the Office vanish'd.    50
    The last hum that it made was that your father
    And Picklock are fall'n out, the man o' law.

PENNYBOY JUNIOR.
    How? This awakes me from my lethargy.

                               *He starts up at this.*

THOMAS BARBER.
    And a great suit is like to be between 'em.
    Picklock denies the feoffment and the trust        55
    Your father says he made of the whole estate
    Unto him, as respecting his mortality,
    When he first laid this late device to try you.

PENNYBOY JUNIOR.
    Has Picklock then a trust?

THOMAS BARBER.               I cannot tell.
    Here comes the worshipful—

[Pennyboy Junior *makes a sign to* Tom, *who hides behind the arras as*] Picklock *enters.*

50. spoil'd] *F;* spoil' *F3.*

---

    39. *dissolv'd*] disintegrated.
    47. *is return'd*] has again become.
    58. *device*] stratagem, plot.

PICKLOCK.                    What, my velvet heir          60
  Turn'd beggar in mind as robes?
PENNYBOY JUNIOR.                    You see what case
  Your and my father's plots have brought me to.
PICKLOCK.
  Your father's you may say indeed, not mine.
  He's a hard-hearted gentleman. I am sorry
  To see his rigid resolution.                              65
  That any man should so put off affection
  And human nature to destroy his own
  And triumph in a victory so cruel.
  He's fall'n out with me for being yours
  And calls me knave, and traitor to his trust,          70
  Says he will have me thrown over the bar—
PENNYBOY JUNIOR.
  Ha' you deserv'd it?
PICKLOCK.                    Oh, good heaven knows
  My conscience and the silly latitude of it!
  A narrow-minded man, my thoughts do dwell
  All in a lane or line indeed, no turning               75
  Nor scarce obliquity in them. I still look
  Right forward to th'intent and scope of that
  Which he would go from now.
PENNYBOY JUNIOR.                    Had you a trust, then?
PICKLOCK.
  Sir, I had somewhat will keep you still lord
  Of all the estate if I be honest as                    80
  I hope I shall. My tender scrupulous breast
  Will not permit me see the heir defrauded
  And like an alien thrust out of the blood.

70. traitor] *F3;* Traytors *F.*

---

61. *case*] with a pun on *case* meaning (1) condition and (2) suit of
clothes.
71. *thrown . . . bar*] disbarred.
73. *silly*] slight.
74. *narrow-minded*] not devious; *OED* incorrectly uses this passage
to exemplify the meaning "illiberal, bigoted."

The laws forbid that I should give consent
To such a civil slaughter of a son.                          85
PENNYBOY JUNIOR.
Where is the deed? Hast thou it with thee?
PICKLOCK.                                            No,
It is a thing of greater consequence
Than to be borne about in a black box
Like a Low-Country *vorloffe* or Welsh brief.
It is at Lickfinger's, under lock and key.                   90
PENNYBOY JUNIOR.
Oh, fetch it hither.
PICKLOCK.                    I have bid him bring it
That you might see it.
PENNYBOY JUNIOR.          Knows he what he brings?
PICKLOCK.
No more than a gardener's ass what roots he carries.
PENNYBOY JUNIOR.
I was a-sending my father, like an ass,
A penitent epistle, but I am glad                            95
I did not now.
PICKLOCK.              Hang him, an austere grape
That has no juice but what is verjuice in him.
PENNYBOY JUNIOR.
I'll show you my letter!
                    Pennyboy [Junior] *runs out to fetch his letter.*
PICKLOCK.                    Show me a defiance!
If I can now commit father and son
And make my profits out of both, commence                    100
A suit with the old man for his whole state
And go to law with the son's credit, undo

92. he brings] *F3;* brings *F.*

---

85. *civil*] legal as opposed to natural.
89. *vorloffe*] leave of absence, furlough (Dutch *forlov*).
89. *Welsh brief*] The Welsh were reputedly very litigious.
97. *verjuice*] juice of unripe grapes or crab apples used like a mild vinegar in cooking.
98. *defiance*] challenge.

Both, both with their own money, it were a piece
Worthy my nightcap and the gown I wear,
A Picklock's name in law. —Where are you, sir?          105
What do you do so long?

[Pennyboy Junior *returns.*]

PENNYBOY JUNIOR.                    I cannot find
Where I have laid it, but I have laid it safe.

PICKLOCK.
No matter, sir, trust you unto my trust.
'Tis that that shall secure you, an absolute deed.
And I confess, it was in trust for you,                  110
Lest anything might have happen'd mortal to him.
But there must be a gratitude thought on,
And aid, sir, for the charges of the suit,
Which will be great, 'gainst such a mighty man
As is our father, and a man possess'd                    115
Of so much land, Pecunia, and her friends.
I am not able to wage law with him,
Yet must maintain the thing as mine own right
Still for your good, and therefore must be bold
To use your credit for monies.

PENNYBOY JUNIOR.                    What thou wilt,       120
So we be safe, and the trust bear it.

PICKLOCK.                    Fear not.
'Tis he must pay arrearages in the end.
We'll milk him and Pecunia, draw their cream down
Before he get the deed into his hands.
My name is Picklock, but he'll find me a padlock.        125

118. mine] *F;* my *F3.*

---

105. *Picklock's name in law*] In discussing "the picklock," Dekker
says that "the *Trade* of Lock-picking may well be called the Black-Art,
for none study it, but those that for other mens goods have sold their
verie soules to the Divell" (*The Bel-man of London,* 1608).
112. *gratitude*] gratuity.
117. *wage law*] go to law.
122. *arrearages*] debts.

[V.ii]                    [*Enter*] Pennyboy Canter.

PENNYBOY CANTER.

    How now? Conferring wi' your learned counsel
    Upo' the cheat? Are you o'the plot to cozen me?

PENNYBOY JUNIOR.

    What plot?

PENNYBOY CANTER. Your counsel knows there, Master Picklock.

    Will you restore the trust yet?

PICKLOCK.                                  Sir, take patience

    And memory unto you and bethink you,                    5
    What trust? Where does't appear? I have your deed.
    Doth your deed specify any trust? Is't not
    A perfect act, and absolute in law,
    Seal'd and deliver'd before witnesses,
    The day and date emergent?

PENNYBOY CANTER.                    But what conference,          10

    What oaths and vows preceded?

PICKLOCK.                                  I will tell you, sir,

    Since I am urg'd, of those. As I remember
    You told me you had got a grown estate
    By griping means, sinisterly.

PENNYBOY CANTER.                    How?

PICKLOCK.                                  And were

    Ev'n weary of it. If the parties lived                    15
    From whom you had wrested it—

PENNYBOY CANTER.                    Ha!

PICKLOCK.                                  You could be glad

    To part with all for satisfaction.
    But since they had yielded to humanity,
    And that just heaven had sent you for a punishment

---

0.1.] Pennyboy Canter, Pennyboy
Junior, Picklock, Thomas Barber.
*F, F3.*

3. S.P. PENNYBOY CANTER.] *1716;*
P. Se. *F, F3.*
6. does't] *F3;* dost *F.*

---

10. *emergent*] casually arising, not especially provided for.
13. *grown*] enormous (de Winter).
14. *griping*] grasping.
14. *sinisterly*] dishonestly.

(You did acknowledge it) this riotous heir                    20
That would bring all to beggary in the end
And daily sow'd consumption where he went—

PENNYBOY CANTER.

You'd cozen both then? Your confederate too?

PICKLOCK.

After a long, mature deliberation,
You could not think where better how to place it—          25

PENNYBOY CANTER.

Than on you, rascal?

PICKLOCK.                    What you please i' your passion.
But with your reason, you will come about
And think a faithful and a frugal friend
To be preferr'd.

PENNYBOY CANTER.     Before a son?

PICKLOCK.                             A prodigal,
A tub without a bottom, as you term'd him.                   30
For which I might return you a vow or two
And seal it with an oath of thankfulness.
I not repent it, neither have I cause. Yet—

PENNYBOY CANTER.

Forehead of steel and mouth of brass! Hath impudence
Polish'd so gross a lie, and dar'st thou vent it?           35
Engine, compos'd of all mix'd metals! Hence!
I will not change a syllab with thee more
Till I may meet thee at a bar in court
Before thy judges.

PICKLOCK.                    Thither it must come
Before I part with it to you, or you, sir.                   40

PENNYBOY CANTER.

I will not hear thee.

PENNYBOY JUNIOR.          Sir, your ear to me though.

                                        *His son entreats him.*

Not that I see through his perplexed plots

---

20. *riotous*] extravagant, prodigal.
36. *mix'd*] impure.
37. *syllab*] syllable.
42. *perplexed*] intricate, complicated.

And hidden ends, nor that my parts depend
Upon the unwinding this so knotted skein
Do I beseech your patience. Unto me                                45
He hath confess'd the trust.

PICKLOCK.                          How? I confess it?

PENNYBOY JUNIOR.
Ay, thou, false man.

PENNYBOY CANTER.        Stand up to him and confront him.

PICKLOCK.
Where? When? To whom?

PENNYBOY JUNIOR.                    To me, even now, and here.
Canst thou deny it?

PICKLOCK.              Can I eat or drink,
Sleep, wake, or dream, arise, sit, go, or stand,                   50
Do anything that's natural?

PENNYBOY JUNIOR.                    Yes, lie
It seems thou canst, and perjure. That is natural!

PICKLOCK.
Oh me! What times are these, of frontless carriage.
An egg o'the same nest! The father's bird!
It runs in a blood, I see.

PENNYBOY JUNIOR.              I'll stop your mouth.             55

PICKLOCK.
With what?

PENNYBOY JUNIOR.    With truth.

PICKLOCK.                          With noise. I must have witness.
Where is your witness? You can produce witness?

PENNYBOY JUNIOR.
As if my testimony were not twenty
Balanc'd with thine.

PICKLOCK.              So say all prodigals,
Sick of self-love, but that's not law, young Scattergood.       60
I live by law.

47. S.P. PENNYBOY CANTER.] *1716;*
P. Se. *F, F3.*

_____

43. *parts*] shares, hence possessions.
50. *go*] walk.
53. *frontless*] shameless.
60. *Scattergood*] a spendthrift character in Cooke's *Greene's Tu
Quoque,* 1611.

PENNYBOY JUNIOR.   Why, if thou hast a conscience,
   That is a thousand witnesses.
PICKLOCK.                          No court
   Grants out a writ of summons for the conscience,
   That I know, nor subpoena nor attachment.
   I must have witness, and of your producing,                65
   Ere this can come to hearing, and it must
   Be heard on oath and witness.
PENNYBOY JUNIOR.                  Come forth, Tom.
           *He produceth* Tom.
   Speak what thou heard'st, the truth, and the whole truth,
   And nothing but the truth.  What said this varlet?
PICKLOCK.
   A rat behind the hangings!
THOMAS BARBER.                   Sir, he said               70
   It was a trust, an act, the which your father
   Had will to alter, but his tender breast
   Would not permit to see the heir defrauded
   And, like an alien, thrust out of the blood.
   The laws forbid that he should give consent             75
   To such a civil slaughter of a son—
PENNYBOY JUNIOR.
   And talk'd of a gratuity to be given
   And aid unto the charges of the suit,
   Which he was to maintain in his own name
   But for my use, he said.
PENNYBOY CANTER.          It is enough.                     80
THOMAS BARBER.
   And he would milk Pecunia and draw down
   Her cream before you got the trust again.
PENNYBOY CANTER.
   Your ears are in my pocket, knave, go shake 'em
   The little while you have them.
PICKLOCK.                        You do trust
   To your great purse.

---

   61–62. *conscience . . . witnesses*] proverb: "Conscience is a thousand
witnesses" (Tilley, C 601).
   83. *Your ears . . . pocket*] Picklock's ears would be cropped when
he was pilloried (see ll. 89–90).

PENNYBOY CANTER.          I ha' you in a purse-net,                    85
　　　Good Master Picklock, wi' your worming brain,
　　　And wriggling engine-head of maintenance,
　　　Which I shall see you hole with, very shortly.
　　　A fine round head, when those two lugs are off,
　　　To trundle through a pillory. You are sure            90
　　　You heard him speak this?
PENNYBOY JUNIOR.              Ay, and more.
THOMAS BARBER.                          Much more.
PICKLOCK.
　　　I'll prove yours maintenance and combination
　　　And sue you all.
PENNYBOY CANTER.     Do, do, my gowned vulture.
　　　Crop in reversion. I shall see you quoited
　　　Over the bar as bargemen do their billets.            95
PICKLOCK.
　　　This 'tis, when men repent of their good deeds
　　　And would ha' 'em in again. They are almost mad,
　　　But I forgive their *lucida intervalla.*
　　　　　　　　　[*Enter* Lickfinger.]
　　　Oh, Lickfinger, come hither. Where's my writing?


[V.iii]
[Picklock *talks with*] Lickfinger [*while*] Young Pennyboy *discovers
it to his father to be his plot of sending for it by the Porter, and
that he is in possession of the deed.*

LICKFINGER.
　　　I sent it you together with your keys.

[V.ii]
99.] *F prints in the margin beginning at l. 99:* "Picklock *spies
Lickfinger, and askes him aside for
the writing.*"

[V.iii]
0.1.] Lickfinger (*to them. F, F3.*
0.1–0.3. Young . . . deed] *F prints
in margin beside ll. 16–24.*

---

85. *purse-net*] bag-shaped net, used for catching rabbits.
87. *maintenance*] wrongfully aiding and abetting litigation.
88. *hole*] go into a hole.
92. *combination*] conspiracy.
[V.iii]
　　0.1. *discovers*] reveals.

PICKLOCK.
How?

LICKFINGER.   By the porter that came for it from you,
And by the token, you had giv'n me the keys,
And bade me bring it.

PICKLOCK.                         And why did you not?

LICKFINGER.
Why did you send a countermand?

PICKLOCK.                              Who, I?                    5

LICKFINGER.
You, or some other you, you put in trust.

PICKLOCK.
In trust?

LICKFINGER.   Your trust's another self, you know,
And without trust, and your trust, how should he
Take notice of your keys or of my charge?

PICKLOCK.
Know you the man?

LICKFINGER.                      I know he was a porter,          10
And a seal'd porter, for he bore the badge
On breast, I am sure.

PICKLOCK.                         I am lost. A plot! I scent it.

LICKFINGER.
Why, and I sent it by the man you sent,
Whom else I had not trusted.

PICKLOCK.                            Plague o' your trust.
I am truss'd up among you.

PENNYBOY JUNIOR.                  Or you may be.                  15

PICKLOCK.
In mine own halter I have made the noose.

                                    Picklock *goes out*.

PENNYBOY JUNIOR.
What was it, Lickfinger?

LICKFINGER.                     A writing, sir,
He sent for't by a token. I was bringing it

12. scent] *F3;* sent *F.*

---

11. *seal'd porter*] member of the Company of Porters.

But that he sent a porter, and he seem'd
A man of decent carriage.

PENNYBOY CANTER.                    'Twas good fortune!                    20
To cheat the cheater was no cheat but justice.
Put off your rags and be yourself again;
This act of piety and good affection
Hath partly reconcil'd me to you.

PENNYBOY JUNIOR.                    Sir—

PENNYBOY CANTER.

No vows, no promises. Too much protestation                    25
Makes that suspected oft, we would persuade.

LICKFINGER.

Hear you the news?

PENNYBOY JUNIOR.        The Office is down. How should we?

LICKFINGER.

But of your uncle?

PENNYBOY JUNIOR.    No.

LICKFINGER.                    He's run mad, sir.

PENNYBOY CANTER.

How, Lickfinger!            *Elder* Pennyboy *startles at the news.*

LICKFINGER.                Stark staring mad, your brother,
H'has almost kill'd his maid—

PENNYBOY CANTER.                    Now heaven forbid.                    30

LICKFINGER.

But that she's cat-liv'd and squirrel-limb'd—
With throwing bed-staves at her. H'has set wide
His outer doors and now keeps open house
For all the passers-by to see his justice.
First, he has apprehended his two dogs                    35
As being o'the plot to cozen him.
And there he sits like an old worm of the peace,
Wrapp'd up in furs, at a square table, screwing,
Examining, and committing the poor curs
To two old cases of close-stools as prisons,                    40

---

32. *bed-staves*] short wooden sticks for tucking in and holding the covering of a bed in place.
38. *screwing*] examining rigorously.

The one of which he calls his Lollard's tower,
Th'other his Block-house, 'cause his two dogs' names
Are Block and Lollard.

PENNYBOY JUNIOR.              This would be brave matter
Unto the jeerers.

PENNYBOY CANTER.      Ay, if so the subject
Were not so wretched.

LICKFINGER.                    Sure, I met them all,                45
I think, upon that quest.

PENNYBOY CANTER.          Faith, like enough.
The vicious still are swift to show their natures.
I'll thither too but with another aim
If all succeed well and my simples take.        [*Exeunt.*]


[V.iv]

*He* [Pennyboy Senior] *is seen sitting at his table, with papers
before him.* [Porter *and the two dogs,* Block *and* Lollard, *are
present.*]

PENNYBOY SENIOR.
Where are the prisoners?

PORTER.                        They are forthcoming, sir,
Or coming forth at least.

PENNYBOY SENIOR.              The rogue is drunk
Since I committed them to his charge. Come hither,
Near me, yet nearer; breathe upon me. (*He smells him.*)
Wine!
Wine, o' my worship, sack, canary sack!                    5

0.1] Pennyboy Senior, Porter. *F*,      0.1–0.2. He . . . him] *F prints in*
*F3.*                                    *margin beside ll. 0.1–1.*

---

[V.iii]
   41. *Lollard's tower*] a name given to a tower at the west end of
St. Paul's next to the Bishop of London's palace and used as the
Bishop's prison for those detected in opinions contrary to the
teachings of the church (Stow, 2:19).
   42. *Block-house*] blockhouse, slang term for prison.
   47. *still*] invariably.
   49. *simples*] medicines made of only one ingredient.
   [V.iv]
   5. *canary sack*] a light sweet wine from the Canaries.

Could not your badge ha' been drunk with fulsome ale,
Or beer, the porter's element? But sack!

PORTER.

I am not drunk. We had, sir, but one pint,
An honest carrier and myself.

PENNYBOY SENIOR.              Who paid for't?

PORTER.

Sir, I did give it him.

PENNYBOY SENIOR.        What, and spend sixpence?      10
A frock spend sixpence? Sixpence!

PORTER.                    Once in a year, sir.

PENNYBOY SENIOR.

In seven years, varlet! Know'st thou what thou hast done,
What a consumption thou hast made of a state?
It might please heaven (a lusty knave and young)
To let thee live some seventy years longer,      15
Till thou art fourscore and ten, perhaps a hundred.
Say seventy years. How many times seven in seventy?
Why, seven times ten is ten times seven. Mark me,
I will demonstrate to thee on my fingers.
Sixpence in seven year (use upon use)      20
Grows in that first seven year to be a twelve-pence.
That, in the next, two shillings; the third, four shillings;
The fourth seven year, eight shillings; the fifth, sixteen;
The sixth, two and thirty; the seventh, three pound four;
The eighth, six pound and eight; the ninth, twelve pound
    sixteen;      25
And the tenth seven, five and twenty pound
Twelve shillings. This thou art fall'n from by thy riot
Shouldst thou live seventy years, by spending sixpence
Once i'the seven. But in a day to waste it!
There is a sum that number cannot reach.      30
Out o' my house, thou pest o' prodigality,
Seed o' consumption! Hence! A wicked keeper
Is oft worse than the prisoners. There's thy penny,

---

6. *fulsome*] abundant, therefore cheap (de Winter).
11. *frock*] a poor man, wearer of a smock-frock.
20. *use upon use*] at compound interest.

Four tokens for thee. Out, away.          [*Exit* Porter.]
              My dogs
May yet be innocent and honest. If not,                    35
I have an entrapping question or two more
To put unto 'em, a cross interr'gatory,
And I shall catch 'em. Lollard, peace!
What whisp'ring was that you had with Mortgage
When you last lick'd her feet? The truth now. Ha!       40
Did you smell she was going? Put down that. And not,
Not to return? You are silent? Good. And when
Leap'd you on Statute? As she went forth? Consent.
There was consent as she was going forth.
'Twould have been fitter at her coming home,             45
But you knew that she would not? To your tower.
You are cunning, are you? I will meet your craft.
Block, show your face, leave your caresses, tell me
And tell me truly, what affronts do you know
Were done Pecunia that she left my house?               50
None? Say you so? Not that you know or will know?
I fear me I shall find you an obstinate cur.
Why did your fellow Lollard cry this morning?
'Cause Broker kick'd him? Why did Broker kick him?
Because he piss'd against my lady's gown?               55
Why, that was no affront, no, no distaste,
You knew o' none? You're a dissembling tyke,
To your hole again, your Block-house. Lollard, arise.
Where did you lift your leg up last, 'gainst what?
Are you struck dummerer now and whine for mercy?       60

37. interr'gatory] *F;* Interrogatory *F3.*
39–42.] *F margin: "Hee calls forth* Lollard, *and examines him."*
45.] *F margin: "He commits him againe."*

47–50.] *F margin: "Calls forth* Blocke, *and examines him."*
48. caresses] *F;* Garesses *F3.*
57.] *F margin: "Commits him."*
59–60.] *F margin: "Lollard is call'd again."*

---

34. *tokens*] farthings.
38. *Lollard, peace!*] "Probably, as in the case of their prototypes in the *Wasps,* Block and Lollard were impersonated by boys dressed as dogs" (de Winter).
57. *tyke*] cur.
60. *dummerer*] beggar who pretended to be mute.

Whose kirtle was't you gnaw'd too, Mistress Band's?
And Wax's stockings? Who? Did Block bescumber
Statute's white suit wi' the parchment lace there
And Broker's satin doublet? All will out.
They had offense, offense enough to quit me.          65
Appear, Block. Fough, 'tis manifest. He shows it.
Should he forswear't, make all the affidavits
Against it that he could afore the bench
And twenty juries, he would be convinc'd.
He bears an air about him doth confess it!          70
To prison again, close prison. Not you, Lollard,
You may enjoy the liberty o'the house.
And yet there is a quirk come in my head,
For which I must commit you too, and close.
Do not repine; it will be better for you.          75

[V.v]

*Enter the jeerers:* Cymbal, Fitton, Shunfield, Almanac, Madrigal.

CYMBAL.

This is enough to make the dogs mad too.
Let's in upon him.
PENNYBOY SENIOR.          How now? What's the matter?
Come you to force the prisoners? Make a rescue?
FITTON.

We come to bail your dogs.

62. stockings] *F;* Stockins *F3.*
66–67.] *F margin:* "Blocke *is sum-*
*on'd the second time.*"
70–71.] *F margin:* "Hee *is re-*
*manded.*"
73–74.] *F margin:* "Lollard *has*
*the liberty of the house.*"

V.v.] *1716;* Act V. Scene II. *F, F3.*
0.1.] Cymbal, Fitton, Shunfield,
Almanac, M a d r i g a l, Pennyboy
Senior, Lickfinger. *F, F3. Mar-*
*ginal note following Scene II:*
"*Enter the* Ieerers." *F.*

---

[V.iv]
    61. *kirtle*] dress made up of a separate bodice and skirt.
    62. *bescumber*] befoul.
    63. *parchment lace*] "lace made of metal thread wound on thin
threads of parchment" or "lace made with needle and thread over
patterns inked in parchment" (Linthicum, p. 134).
    69. *convinc'd*] convicted.
    73. *quirk*] sudden turn of thought.

PENNYBOY SENIOR.                    They are not bailable.
They stand committed without bail or mainprise.                    5
Your bail cannot be taken.
SHUNFIELD.                    Then the truth is
We come to vex you.
ALMANAC.                    Jeer you.
MADRIGAL.                    Bait you rather.
CYMBAL.
A baited usurer will be good flesh.
FITTON.
And tender, we are told.
PENNYBOY SENIOR.                    Who is the butcher
Amongst you that is come to cut my throat?                    10
SHUNFIELD.
You would die a calf's death fain, but 'tis an ox's
Is meant you.
FITTON.                    To be fairly knock'd o'the head,
SHUNFIELD.
With a good jeer or two.
PENNYBOY SENIOR.                    And from your jawbone,
Don Assinigo?
CYMBAL.                    Shunfield, a jeer, you have it.
SHUNFIELD.
I do confess a washing blow. But snarl,                    15
You that might play the third dog, for your teeth,
You ha' no money now.
FITTON.                    No, nor no Mortgage—
ALMANAC.
Nor Band—

---

5. *without . . . mainprise*] unable to obtain release by finding sureties.

8–9. *baited . . . butcher*] Baited bull was believed to be more tender and nutritious than animals slaughtered without baiting.

8. *baited usurer*] tormented usurer, with a pun on "bated" usurer, that is, a usurer who has lost weight (see l. 44 below) and an ironic echo of Pennyboy Senior's "bate of the use" at III.iv.42.

13–14. *jawbone . . . Assinigo*] Samson slew a thousand Philistines with the jawbone of an ass (Judges 15:15–17).

14. *Assinigo*] a little ass, a foolish fellow (Span. *asnico*).

15. *washing*] swashing, slashing with great force (fencing).

MADRIGAL.            Nor Statute—

CYMBAL.                        No, nor blushet Wax.

PENNYBOY SENIOR.

    Nor you no Office, as I take it.

SHUNFIELD.                          Cymbal,

    A mighty jeer.

FITTON.            Pox o'these true jests, I say.            20

MADRIGAL.

    He will turn the better jeerer.

ALMANAC.                          Let's upon him,

    And if we cannot jeer him down in wit—

MADRIGAL.

    Let's do't in noise.

SHUNFIELD.            Content.

MADRIGAL.                          Charge, man o' war.

ALMANAC.

    Lay him aboard.

SHUNFIELD.            We'll gi' him a broadside first.

FITTON.

    Where's your venison now?

CYMBAL.                          Your red-deer pies?            25

SHUNFIELD.

    Wi' your bak'd turkeys?

ALMANAC.            And your partridges?

MADRIGAL.

    Your pheasants and fat swans?

PENNYBOY SENIOR.                    Like you, turn'd geese.

MADRIGAL.

    But such as will not keep your capitol!

SHUNFIELD.

    You were wont to ha' your breams—

ALMANAC.                          And trouts sent in—

CYMBAL.

    Fat carps and salmons—

FITTON.            Ay, and now and then,            30

---

    24. *Lay him aboard*] come alongside him to fight.

    27–28. *geese . . . capitol!*] a reference to the tradition that the cackling of the sacred geese warned the Romans that the Gauls were attempting to scale the Capitol (390 B.C.)

An emblem o' yourself, an o'ergrown pike.

PENNYBOY SENIOR.

You are a Jack, sir.

FITTON.                         You ha' made a shift

To swallow twenty such poor Jacks ere now.

ALMANAC.

If he should come to feed upon poor John—

MADRIGAL.

Or turn pure Jack-a-Lent after all this.                    35

FITTON.

Tut, he'll live like a grasshopper—

MADRIGAL.                         On dew.

SHUNFIELD.

Or like a bear, with licking his own claws.

CYMBAL.

Ay, if his dogs were away.

ALMANAC.                         He'll eat them first

While they are fat.

FITTON.                         Faith, and when they are gone,

Here's nothing to be seen beyond—

CYMBAL.                                     Except        40

His kindred, spiders, natives o'the soil.

ALMANAC.

Dust he will ha' enough here to breed fleas—

MADRIGAL.

But by that time he'll ha' no blood to rear 'em.

---

42. enough here] *F;* enough *F3.*

---

31. *pike*] voracious fish, also known as a jack.

33. *poor Jacks*] dried hake.

34. *poor John*] another name for poor Jack.

35. *Jack-a-Lent*] a stuffed puppet set up to be pelted from Ash Wednesday to Good Friday and then burned.

36–37. *live . . . claws*] Pliny observes of the grasshopper: "This is the only living creature actually without a mouth. . . . they live on dew" (11. 32, pp. 489, 491). During hibernation bears "live by sucking their forepaws" (8. 54, p. 91).

42.] Pliny says that some insects "are generated out of dirt by the rays of the sun, creatures that hop with a frisk of their hind legs" (11. 39, p. 503).

SHUNFIELD.

    He will be as thin as a lantern; we shall see through him—

ALMANAC.

    And his gut colon, tell his *intestina*—               45

PENNYBOY SENIOR.

    Rogues! Rascals!         *His dogs bark: (bow wow).*

FITTON.          He calls his dogs to his aid.

ALMANAC.

    Oh, they but rise at mention of his tripes.

CYMBAL.

    Let them alone. They do it not for him.

MADRIGAL.

    They bark *se defendendo.*

SHUNFIELD.               Or for custom,

    As commonly curs do, one for another.          50

              [*Enter* Lickfinger.]

LICKFINGER.

    Arm, arm you, gentlemen jeerers, th'old Canter

    Is coming in upon you with his forces,

    The gentleman that was the Canter.

SHUNFIELD.               Hence!

FITTON.

    Away!

CYMBAL.    What is he?

ALMANAC.          Stay not to ask questions.

FITTON.

    He's a flame.

SHUNFIELD.     A furnace.

ALMANAC.          A consumption,        55

    Kills where he goes.        *They all run away.*

LICKFINGER.       See! the whole covey is scatter'd.

    'Ware, 'ware the hawk. I love to see him fly.

57. hawk] *Whalley* (*H.S. mark
this reading* Editor); Hawkes *F,
F3.*

---

49. *se defendendo*] in self-defense.

57. *'Ware . . . hawk*] proverbial (Tilley, H 227). Tilley notes that
it is "a phrase applied to an officer of the law, who pounced upon
criminals."

[V.vi]
[*Enter*] Pennyboy Canter, Pennyboy Junior, Pecunia [, Statute,
Band, Wax *and* Mortgage].

PENNYBOY CANTER.

    You see by this amazement and distraction
    What your companions were, a poor, affrighted,
    And guilty race of men that dare to stand
    No breath of truth, but conscious to themselves
    Of their no-wit, or honesty, ran routed          5
    At every panic terror themselves bred.
    Where else, as confident as sounding brass,
    Their tinkling captain, Cymbal, and the rest,
    Dare put on any visor to deride
    The wretched, or with buffoon license, jest     10
    At whatsoe'er is serious, if not sacred.

PENNYBOY SENIOR.

    Who's this? My brother, and restor'd to life?

PENNYBOY CANTER.

    Yes, and sent hither to restore your wits
    If your short madness be not more than anger
    Conceived for your loss, which I return you.     15
    See here, your Mortgage, Statute, Band, and Wax,
    Without your Broker, come to abide with you
    And vindicate the prodigal from stealing
    Away the lady. Nay, Pecunia herself
    Is come to free him fairly and discharge     20
    All ties but those of love unto her person,
    To use her like a friend, not like a slave
    Or like an idol. Superstition
    Doth violate the deity it worships
    No less than scorn doth. And believe it, brother,    25
    The use of things is all, and not the store:

0.1–0.2.] Pennyboy Canter, Penny-    10. buffoon] *F3;* buffon *F.*
boy Senior, Pennyboy Junior, Pe-    12–15.] *F margin:* "Peny-boy Se.
cunia, Train. *F, F3.*    *acknowledgeth his elder brother."*

---

   7–8. *sounding . . . Cymbal*] See Persons of the Play, 1. 4, note.
   14.] Horace defines anger as a brief madness (*Epistles* 1.2.62).

Surfeit and fulness have kill'd more than famine.
The sparrow with his little plumage flies
While the proud peacock, overcharg'd with pens,
Is fain to sweep the ground with his grown train          30
And load of feathers.

PENNYBOY SENIOR.                Wise and honor'd brother,
None but a brother and sent from the dead,
As you are to me, could have altered me.
I thank my destiny, that is so gracious.
Are there no pains, no penalties decreed                   35
From whence you come, to us that smother money
In chests and strangle her in bags?

PENNYBOY CANTER.                            Oh, mighty,
Intolerable fines, and mulcts impos'd
(Of which I come to warn you), forfeitures
Of whole estates, if they be known and taken!              40

PENNYBOY SENIOR.

I thank you, brother, for the light you have given me.
I will prevent 'em all. First free my dogs,
Lest what I ha' done to them (and against law)
Be a praemunire. For by Magna Carta
They could not be committed as close prisoners,            45
My learned counsel tells me here, my cook,
And yet he show'd me the way first.

LICKFINGER.                                Who did? I?
I trench the liberty o'the subjects?

44. praemunire] *F3;* Premuniri *F.*

---

29. *pens]* feathers.
35. *pains]* punishments.
38. *mulcts]* fines or penalties.
44. *praemunire]* the offense of taking a case to a court outside the jurisdiction of the Crown; it was punishable chiefly by forfeiture.
46–48. *My . . . subjects?]* a punning allusion to Sir Edward Coke, one of the "patriots" in the House of Commons, who actively championed "the liberty o'the subjects." See I.Intermean.60, note, and footnote 10 of the Introduction.
48. *trench]* encroach on.

PENNYBOY CANTER.                        Peace.

Picklock your guest, that stentor, hath infected you,
Whom I have safe enough in a wooden collar.                    50

PENNYBOY SENIOR.

Next, I restore these servants to their lady
With freedom, heart of cheer, and countenance.
It is their year and day of jubilee.

STATUTE. BAND. WAX. MORTGAGE.

We thank you, sir.

PENNYBOY SENIOR.        And lastly, to my nephew,

I give my house, goods, lands, all but my vices,                    55
And those I go to cleanse, kissing this lady,
Whom I do give him too, and join their hands.

PENNYBOY CANTER.

If the spectators will join theirs, we thank 'em.

PENNYBOY JUNIOR.

And wish they may, as I, enjoy Pecunia.

PECUNIA.

And so Pecunia herself doth wish,                    60
That she may still be aid unto their uses,
Not slave unto their pleasures or a tyrant
Over their fair desires, but teach them all
The golden mean: the prodigal how to live,
The sordid and the covetous how to die:                    65
That, with sound mind; this, safe frugality.        [*Exeunt.*]

## THE END

54. S.P. STATUTE . . . MORTGAGE.]        55–56.] F margin: *"Her Traine*
*this edn.;* TRA. *F, F3.*                        *thanks him."*

---

49. *stentor*] "Stentor of the brazen voice, whose voice is as the voice
of fifty other men," *Iliad* 5.785–86.

50. *wooden collar*] pillory.

52–53. *freedom . . . jubilee*] In biblical times, the year of jubilee
was "a year of emancipation and restoration . . . during it . . . Hebrew
slaves were to be set free, and [certain] lands and houses . . . that
had been sold were to revert to their former owners or their heirs"
(*OED*).

53. *jubilee*] refers to 1625, the date of composition of the play; in
the seventeenth century, a jubilee was celebrated every twenty-five
years.

# THE EPILOGUE

Thus have you seen the maker's double scope,
To profit and delight, wherein our hope
Is, though the clout we do not always hit,
It will not be imputed to his wit!
A tree so tried and bent as 'twill not start.                5
Nor doth he often crack a string of art,
Though there may other accidents as strange
Happen; the weather of your.looks may change,
Or some high wind of misconceit arise
To cause an alteration in our skies.                         10
If so, we are sorry that have so misspent
Our time and tackle, yet he is confident
And vows the next fair day, he'll have us shoot
The same match o'er for him if you'll come to't.

---

11. we are] *F;* w'are *F3.*          12. he is] *F;* he's *F3.*

---

1. *maker's*] Cf. "The Prologue for the Stage," l. 5, note.
2. *To profit and delight*] part of the Horatian motto on the title page.
3. *clout*] wooden pin which fastened the archery target to the butt (Fr. *clou*).
5. *tree*] bow.
9. *misconceit*] misconception.

# Appendix

## Chronology

Approximate years are indicated by *, occurrences in doubt by (?).

<table>
<tr><td>Political and Literary Events</td><td>Life and Works of Ben Jonson</td></tr>
</table>

1558
Accession of Queen Elizabeth I.
Robert Greene born.
Thomas Kyd born.
Thomas Lodge born.

1560
George Chapman born.

1561
Francis Bacon born.

1564
Shakespeare born.
Christopher Marlowe born.

1567
Thomas Nashe born.

1572
Thomas Dekker born.*
John Donne born.
St. Bartholomew's Day Massacre.

1573

Benjamin Jonson born in London, about June 11, posthumous son of a clergyman. His mother remarried a bricklayer.

1574
Thomas Heywood born.*
Cyril Tourneur born.*
John Webster born.*

1575
Two Dutch Anabaptists burned at the stake in England.

1576

The Theatre, the first permanent public theater in London, established by James Burbage.
John Marston born.

1577

The Curtain theater opened.
Holinshed's *Chronicles of England, Scotland and Ireland.*
Drake begins circumnavigation of the earth; completed 1580.

1578

John Lyly's *Euphues: The Anatomy of Wit.*

1579

John Fletcher born.
Sir Thomas North's translation of Plutarch's *Lives.*

1580

Thomas Middleton born.

1583

Philip Massinger born.

1584

Francis Beaumont born.*

1586

Death of Sir Philip Sidney.
John Ford born.
Kyd's *THE SPANISH TRAGEDY.*

1587

The Rose theater opened by Henslowe.
Marlowe's *TAMBURLAINE*, Part I.*
Execution of Mary, Queen of Scots.
Drake raids Cadiz.

Attends Westminster School, studying under William Camden, one of the most learned men in England.*

1588

Defeat of the Spanish Armada.
Marlowe's *TAMBURLAINE*, Part II.*

Leaves Westminster School; apprenticed as a bricklayer.*

APPENDIX

1589
Greene's *FRIAR BACON AND FRIAR BUNGAY.**
Marlowe's *THE JEW OF MAL- TA.**

1590
Spenser's *Faerie Queene* (Books I–III) published.
Sidney's *Arcadia* published.
Shakespeare's *HENRY VI, Parts I–III,* *TITUS ANDRONICUS.**

1591
Shakespeare's *RICHARD III.**

Serves as a soldier in the Low Countries (1591–1592).

1592
Marlowe's *DOCTOR FAUSTUS** and *EDWARD II.**
Shakespeare's *TAMING OF THE SHREW** and *THE COMEDY OF ERRORS.**
Death of Greene.

1593
Shakespeare's *LOVE'S LABOR'S LOST;** *Venus and Adonis* published.
Death of Marlowe.
Theaters closed on account of plague.

1594
Shakespeare's *TWO GENTLE- MEN OF VERONA;** *The Rape of Lucrece* published.
Shakespeare's company becomes Lord Chamberlain's Men.
Death of Kyd.

Marries Anne Lewis.

1595
The Swan theater built.
Sidney's *Defense of Poesy* published.
Shakespeare's *ROMEO AND JU- LIET,** *A MIDSUMMER*

Serves as an actor in one of the London companies.**

*NIGHT'S DREAM,\* RICHARD II.\**
Raleigh's first expedition to Guiana.

1596
Spenser's *Faerie Queene* (Books IV–VI) published.
Shakespeare's *MERCHANT OF VENICE,\* KING JOHN.\**
James Shirley born.

Collaborated on plays, some for the Admiral's Men.\*

1597
Bacon's *Essays* (first edition).
Shakespeare's *HENRY IV,* Part I.\*

Imprisoned for part authorship of a lost play, *THE ISLE OF DOGS.*

1598
Demolition of The Theatre.
Shakespeare's *MUCH ADO ABOUT NOTHING,\* HENRY IV,* Part II.\*
Seven books of Chapman's translation of Homer's *Iliad* published.

*THE CASE IS ALTERED* (Children of Chapel Royal).\*
*EVERY MAN IN HIS HUMOR* (Lord Chamberlain's Men).
Kills Gabriel Spencer, a fellow actor, in a duel: imprisoned but freed on plea of benefit of clergy; converted to Roman Catholicism while in jail.

1599
The Paul's Boys reopen their theater.
The Globe theater opened.
Shakespeare's *AS YOU LIKE IT,\* HENRY V, JULIUS CAESAR.\**
Marston's *ANTONIO AND MELLIDA,\** Parts I and II.
Dekker's *THE SHOEMAKER'S HOLIDAY.\**
Death of Spenser.

*EVERY MAN OUT OF HIS HUMOR* (Lord Chamberlain's Men) starts a vogue in satiric comedy.

1600
Shakespeare's *TWELFTH NIGHT.\**
The Fortune theater built by Alleyn.
The Children of the Chapel begin to play at the Blackfriars.

*CYNTHIA'S REVELS* (Children of Chapel Royal).

1601

Shakespeare's *HAMLET,* MERRY WIVES OF WINDSOR.*
Insurrection and execution of the Earl of Essex.

*POETASTER* (Children of Chapel Royal).
Publicly feuds with Marston and Dekker in the War of the Theaters.

1602

Shakespeare's *TROILUS AND CRESSIDA.*
*THE MERRY DEVIL OF EDMONTON.*

1603

Death of Queen Elizabeth I: accession of James VI of Scotland as James I.
Florio's translation of Montaigne's *Essays* published.
Shakespeare's *ALL'S WELL THAT ENDS WELL.*
Heywood's *A WOMAN KILLED WITH KINDNESS.*
Marston's *THE MALCONTENT.*
Shakespeare's company becomes the King's Men.
Sir Kenelm Digby born.

*SEJANUS* (King's Men) hissed off the stage.
Son Benjamin dies, aged six.
Forms "The Mermaid Club" and gathers a coterie about him.

1604

Shakespeare's *MEASURE FOR MEASURE,* OTHELLO.*
Marston's *THE FAWN.*
Chapman's *BUSSY D'AMBOIS.*

1605

Shakespeare's *KING LEAR.*
Marston's *THE DUTCH COURTESAN.*
Bacon's *Advancement of Learning* published.
The Gunpowder Plot.

Early masque at court, *THE MASQUE OF BLACKNESS.*
*EASTWARD HO,* in collaboration with Chapman and Marston (Children of the Queen's Revels); Jonson and Chapman imprisoned because of alleged derogatory allusions to King James.

1606

Shakespeare's *MACBETH.*
Tourneur's *REVENGER'S TRAGEDY.*

*VOLPONE* (King's Men).*

The Red Bull theater built.
Death of John Lyly.

1607
Shakespeare's *ANTONY AND CLEOPATRA.**
Beaumont's *KNIGHT OF THE BURNING PESTLE.**
Settlement of Jamestown, Virginia.

*VOLPONE* performed at Oxford and Cambridge.*

1608
Shakespeare's *CORIOLANUS,** *TIMON OF ATHENS,** *PERICLES.**
Chapman's *CONSPIRACY AND TRAGEDY OF CHARLES, DUKE OF BYRON.**
Richard Burbage leases Blackfriars Theater for King's company.
John Milton born.

1609
Shakespeare's *CYMBELINE;** *Sonnets* published.
Dekker's *Gull's Hornbook* published.

*EPICOENE* (Children of the Queen's Revels).

1610
Chapman's *REVENGE OF BUSSY D'AMBOIS.**
Richard Crashaw born.

*THE ALCHEMIST* (King's Men). Returns to Anglican religion.*

1611
Authorized (King James) Version of the Bible published.
Shakespeare's *THE WINTER'S TALE,** *TIIE TEMPEST.**
Beaumont and Fletcher's *A KING AND NO KING.*
Middleton's *A CHASTE MAID IN CHEAPSIDE.**
Tourneur's *ATHEIST'S TRAGEDY.**
Chapman's translation of *Iliad* completed.

*CATILINE* (King's Men) damned by theater audiences, but later greatly respected by readers. Writing masqucs for Court cntertainments regularly up to 1625.

1612
Webster's *THE WHITE DEVIL.* *  Travels in France as tutor to son
of Sir Walter Raleigh (1612–1613).

1613
The Globe theater burned.
Shakespeare's *HENRY VIII* (with
Fletcher).
Webster's *THE DUCHESS OF
MALFI.* *
Sir Thomas Overbury murdered.

1614
The Globe theater rebuilt.         *BARTHOLOMEW FAIR* (Lady
The Hope Theatre built.            Elizabeth's Men).

1616
Chapman's *Whole Works of*         *THE DEVIL IS AN ASS* (King's
*Homer.*                           Men).
Death of Shakespeare.              Publication of Folio edition of
Death of Beaumont.                 *Works* ridiculed for its pretension.
                                   Receives royal pension, and hence-
                                   forth he is considered poet laure-
                                   ate, although he never styled him-
                                   self such.

1618
Outbreak of Thirty Years War.      Journeys on foot to Scotland;
Execution of Raleigh.              visits there with William Drum-
                                   mond (1618–1619).

1619                               Given honorary M.A. by Oxford
                                   University.

1620
Settlement of Plymouth, Massa-
chusetts.

1621
Middleton's *WOMEN BEWARE
WOMEN.* *
Robert Burton's *Anatomy of Mel-
ancholy* published.
Andrew Marvell born.

1622
Middleton and Rowley's *THE
CHANGELING.* *
Henry Vaughan born.

1623
Publication of Folio edition of Shakespeare's *COMEDIES, HISTORIES, AND TRAGEDIES.*

Lectures on rhetoric at Gresham College in London(?).
Books and manuscripts lost when lodgings burn.

1625
Death of King James I; accession of Charles I.
Death of Fletcher.

1626
Death of Tourneur.
Death of Bacon.

*THE STAPLE OF NEWS* (King's Men).

1627
Death of Middleton.

1628
Ford's *THE LOVER'S MELANCHOLY.*
Petition of Right.
Buckingham assassinated.

Paralyzed by a stroke.
Appointed chronologer of the City of London.

1629

*THE NEW INN* (King's Men).

1631
Shirley's *THE TRAITOR.*
Death of Donne.
John Dryden born.

Quarrels with Inigo Jones.

1632
Massinger's *THE CITY MADAM.*\*

*THE MAGNETIC LADY* (King's Men).

1633
Donne's *Poems* published.
Death of George Herbert.

*A TALE OF A TUB,* revised from an earlier play (Queen Henrietta's Men).

1634
Death of Chapman, Marston, Webster.\*
Publication of *THE TWO NOBLE KINSMEN,* with title-page attribution to Shakespeare and Fletcher.
Milton's *Comus.*

A final "entertainment," *LOVE'S WELCOME AT BOLSOVER.*

1635
Sir Thomas Browne's *Religio Medici.*

1637

Jonson dies in Westminster, August 6; buried in Westminster Abbey, August 9.

1638

*Jonsonus Virbius,* a memorial volume, published.

1639
First Bishops' War.
Death of Carew.*

1640
Short Parliament.
Long Parliament impeaches Laud.
Death of Massinger, Burton.

*Works* published, two volumes, folio, by Sir Kenelm Digby, (1640–1641).

1641
Irish rebel.
Death of Heywood.

1642
Charles I leaves London; Civil War breaks out.
Shirley's *COURT SECRET.*
All theaters closed by Act of Parliament.

1643
Parliament swears to the Solemn League and Convenant.

1645
Ordinance for New Model Army enacted.

1646
End of First Civil War.

1647
Army occupies London.
Charles I forms alliance with Scots.
Publication of Folio edition of Beaumont and Fletcher's *COMEDIES AND TRAGEDIES.*

1648
Second Civil War.

1649
Execution of Charles I.

1650
Jeremy Collier born.

1651
Hobbes' *Leviathan* published.

1652
First Dutch War begins (ended 1654).
Thomas Otway born.

1653
Nathaniel Lee born.*

1656
D'Avenant's *THE SIEGE OF RHODES* performed at Rutland House.

1657
John Dennis born.

1658
Death of Oliver Cromwell.
D'Avenant's *THE CRUELTY OF THE SPANIARDS IN PERU* performed at the Cockpit.

1660
Restoration of Charles II.
Theatrical patents granted to Thomas Killigrew and Sir William D'Avenant, authorizing them to form, respectively, the King's and the Duke of York's Companies.

1661
Cowley's *THE CUTTER OF COLEMAN STREET*.
D'Avenant's *THE SIEGE OF RHODES* (expanded to two parts).

1662
Charter granted to the Royal Society.

1663
Dryden's *THE WILD GALLANT*.
Tuke's *THE ADVENTURES OF FIVE HOURS*.

1664
Sir John Vanbrugh born.
Dryden's *THE RIVAL LADIES.*
Dryden and Howard's *THE IN-
DIAN QUEEN.*
Etherege's *THE COMICAL RE-
VENGE.*

1665
Second Dutch War begins (ended
1667).
Great Plague.
Dryden's *THE INDIAN EM-
PEROR.*
Orrery's *MUSTAPHA.*

1666
Fire of London.
Death of James Shirley.